God's Promises for Our Children

Raising Godly Children in a Broken World and Praying Home the Prodigal

By

William Nelson

Accept Jesus as Your Lord and Savior

Dedication

To all the mothers, fathers, and grandparents, I've been honored to unite my faith with you through prayer for the salvation of your wayward sons, daughters, and grandchildren. Jeremiah 31:16 "... they shall come back from the land of the enemy." (NKJV)

Acknowledgements

First, I give all glory and honor to God and to Jesus Christ, my Lord and Savior. He is the source of every promise and the faithful Father to all generations. Without His Word, His Spirit, and His constant love, this book would not exist. His promises are unwavering, His mercy never ends, and His heart for our children is deeper than we can comprehend.

To my wife, June—thank you for faithfully standing beside me in every season. Your belief in God's calling on my life and your partnership in the vision for this book have been invaluable. Your prayers, wisdom, and quiet strength have encouraged me more than I could ever express. You've raised your children in the truth and, by your example, inspired others to do the same.

To my children and grandchildren—Audra, Tyler, Dylan, and Avery—you are the living evidence of God's goodness. Your lives inspired many of the prayers and promises written on these pages. My most profound hope is that what you read here will guide your steps and ground your hearts in the truth of God's Word.

To every parent, grandparent, and family member who desires to see their children walk in God's truth—this book is for you. Thank you for your faith, perseverance, and commitment to standing on God's promises. Your stories and faith journey helped shape this book into something practical and deeply rooted in Scripture.

To Pastor Doyle Haire, who led me to surrender my life to Christ at a young age—thank you. And to Pastor Caldwell, Jerry Ross, and Gary Blunier—your belief in me and your willingness to mentor and encourage me have made a lasting impact. Your dedication to the Gospel and to building up others in their calling has been a blessing to my life.

To those behind the scenes—editors, designers, prayer partners, and friends—thank you for your role in bringing this book to completion. Your excellence and faithfulness are reflected in every page, and your contributions have helped carry this message further than I could have.

To Pat Salsbury—thank you for standing with me during some of my most difficult times. Your friendship, encouragement, and unwavering support helped me when I needed it most. I realize I never thanked you as I should have, and for that, I apologize. Your prayers and willingness to help, no matter the time or circumstance, have meant more to me than words can say. Thank you.

And finally, to you—the reader—thank you for picking up this book with a heart full of hope and faith. May you be reminded that God's Word never fails. His promises are to you and for your children. As you pray, believe, and speak His Word over your family, may you see His faithfulness unfold before your eyes. We stand together on the unshakable promises of God—for they belong to every generation.

—William Nelson

About the Author

William Nelson, a United States Air Force veteran, lives with his wife, June, in Little Rock, Arkansas. After completing his military service, William earned a bachelor of science from the University of Arkansas and pursued two years of postgraduate Bible Studies. His educational background and deep personal faith have shaped a lifelong passion for studying and sharing God's Word.

William writes as an author and speaker with clarity, warmth, and conviction. His message is rooted in the belief that God's promises are as powerful and relevant today as they were in biblical times. Whether addressing themes of healing, restoration, or faith for future generations, William's work speaks directly to the heart of those seeking to live with purpose and trust in God's enduring truth.

In *God's Promises for Our Children*, William speaks to parents and families with conviction, pointing them to Scripture as the unshakable foundation for raising godly children. A veteran of the United States Air Force and deeply rooted in his Christian faith, William combines biblical insight with a passion for equipping others to stand on God's Word. He works for a global marriage and family ministry, supporting families in building Christ-centered homes. His passion is to help people encounter the life-changing power of God's promises through Jesus Christ, the same yesterday, today, and forever.

Through his books, ministry, and personal life, William Nelson is committed to leaving a legacy of faith, hope, and truth for future generations.

Table of Contents

Introduction

In a world growing ever more unpredictable, where darkness and confusion seem to lurk around every corner, there remains one steadfast truth that anchors the hearts of believing parents: God is faithful to His promises. That truth becomes the heartbeat of this book. *God's Promises for Our Children* is not merely a reflection on comforting Scripture; it is a call to intentional parenting through prayer, faith, and the unshakable confidence that God's Word is eternal, alive, and able to perform what He has spoken.

From the very beginning, God has demonstrated a deep concern for families and generations. When He made a covenant with Abraham, it was not just for the man himself but for his descendants as well. "And I will establish My covenant between Me and you and your descendants after you in their generations, for an everlasting covenant, to be God to you and your descendants after you" (Genesis 17:7, NKJV). The generational nature of God's promises is not incidental—it is intentional. This should awaken hope in every parent who dares to believe that the promises of God do not end with them but extend to their children and grandchildren.

This book was written to help you, the parent, grandparent, guardian, or mentor, learn how to stand in faith over the lives of your children, declaring the Word of God boldly and consistently. Our children live in a culture that often undermines the truth, questions identity, and challenges morality. Yet, we have been given a powerful weapon: the living Word of God. "For the word of God is living and powerful, and sharper than any two-edged sword" (Hebrews 4:12, NKJV). When we speak God's promises, we aren't merely expressing hopeful wishes—we are aligning ourselves with divine truth and calling heaven's purposes into the lives of those we love.

Many parents carry the weight of fear: fear of what the world might do to their children, fear that their prayers aren't enough, fear that their pasts might hinder the future of their kids. But God has not called us to parent from a place of fear. His Word says, "For God has not given us a spirit of fear, but of power and love and a sound mind" (2 Timothy 1:7, NKJV). This means that our role as spiritual protectors and leaders in the home is to be done in confidence, equipped by God's Spirit, and empowered by His truth.

If you have ever felt helpless watching your child struggle—whether physically, emotionally, or spiritually—know this: you are not helpless. God equips you to stand in the gap. One of the most profound examples of intercession is found in the Book of Job. Speaking of his daily practice, Job said, "He would rise early in the morning and offer burnt offerings according to the number of them all. For Job said, 'It may be that my sons have sinned and cursed God in their hearts.' Thus Job did regularly" (Job 1:5, NKJV). 'Job's love compelled him to intercede on behalf of his children. You can do the same, not with burnt offerings, but with the declarations of 'God's Word and prayers of faith.

We are called to be spiritual watchmen over our households. Just as Nehemiah stood on the wall to guard the people from their enemies, we, too, must watch and pray. "Nevertheless we made our prayer to our God, and because of them, we set a watch against them day and night" (Nehemiah 4:9, NKJV). Our prayers are not passive; they are strategic acts of war against the forces that seek to harm our children. With each promise of God declared over their lives, we build a wall of spiritual protection.

'God's promises are not vague, generalized blessings; they are specific, powerful truths spoken from the heart of the Father to His children. These promises cover every area of our 'children's lives—salvation, health, wisdom, purpose, peace, and protection. When we declare these truths over them, we are not only reminding ourselves of God's character—we are inviting His divine presence to shape their futures. "So shall My word be that goes forth from My mouth; it shall not return to Me void, but it shall accomplish what I please, and it shall prosper in the thing for which I sent it" (Isaiah 55:11, NKJV).

One of the most comforting aspects of 'God's promises is that they are not dependent on our perfection. As parents, we will make mistakes. We will have days when we are overwhelmed, exhausted, or unsure. But God's covenant is not built on our performance—it is built on His faithfulness. "The steadfast love of the Lord never ceases; His mercies never come to an end; they are new every morning; great is Your faithfulness" (Lamentations 3:22–23, ESV). What a joy it is to know that even when we fall short, God does not. His promises remain.

As you begin this journey through God's promises for our children, I encourage you to pray boldly, speak truthfully, and believe deeply. The Bible is not a book of ancient sayings; it is the voice of God that speaks directly to our modern lives and the hearts of our children. "All Scripture is given by inspiration of God, and is profitable for doctrine, for reproof, for correction, for instruction in righteousness" (2 Timothy 3:16, NKJV).

This book will walk you through many inspired Scriptures, categorized by topic. You may wish to focus on one promise at a time, meditating on it daily, speaking it over your children, and writing it in journals or on note cards. Repetition is powerful. God told His people to keep His Word ever before them, saying, "You shall teach them diligently to your children, and shall talk of them when you sit in your house when you walk by the way when you lie down, and when you rise up" (Deuteronomy 6:7, NKJV). The more our children hear the truth, the more likely it is to shape their thinking and their decisions.

Whether your child is an infant, a teenager, or an adult, your words still carry weight. Your prayers still have power. No distance in the spirit realm hinders the hand of God. He sees every heart, hears every cry, and responds to every prayer rooted in faith. "The effective, fervent prayer of a righteous man avails much" (James 5:16, NKJV).

You may feel at times that 'you're fighting against a tide of negativity, rebellion, or spiritual warfare. Take heart—you're not alone. God fights with you and for you. "The Lord will fight for you, and you shall hold your peace" (Exodus 14:14, NKJV). The spiritual battle for your children's lives is real, but so is the power of God. You are not praying empty prayers into the air; you are speaking with the authority of heaven, declaring 'God's truth in a world full of lies.

There is something beautiful about hearing a child repeat the Word of God. When you teach your children to speak Scripture, you are not only arming them for life—you are writing eternity on their hearts. God promised, "I will put My law in their minds, and write it on their hearts; and I will be their God, and they shall be My people" (Jeremiah 31:33, NKJV). This divine imprint is stronger than anything the world could offer.

Even if your children have wandered from God or are currently resisting the truth, never stop praying. Never stop declaring. The seeds you plant today will bear fruit in due season. "Train up a child in the way he should go, and when he is old, he will not depart from it" (Proverbs 22:6, NKJV). 'God's promises are not limited by time—they are eternal. What may seem delayed is not denied. Keep believing. Keep standing. Keep speaking.

Our children are precious in God's sight. He sees them, knows them, and has a plan for their lives. "Before I formed you in the womb I knew you; before you were born I sanctified you" (Jeremiah 1:5, NKJV). Every child is born with a purpose, and every parent has the privilege of calling that purpose forth through faith. You are not just raising children; you are raising world changers, kingdom builders, and vessels of God's glory.

Several scriptures are repeated throughout this book because each repetition offers a fresh perspective or a deeper understanding of their meaning. Just as a diamond reflects different colors when viewed from various angles, these scriptures reveal new insights depending on the context in which they are examined; by examining them from various perspectives—whether historical, spiritual, personal, or practical—their relevance becomes clearer and more applicable to different aspects of life. This repetition is intentional, reinforcing key messages while inviting the reader to engage with the scriptures in a more profound and transformative way.

Let this book be a guide as you seek the Lord on behalf of your children. Let each promise serve as a building block in your family's spiritual foundation. Let your heart be stirred with renewed confidence in the power of God's Word. May your faith rise with every page, and may your home be filled with the presence and peace of the Lord.

As you move into the chapters ahead, don't rush. Soak in each Scripture. Speak it aloud. Write it down. Let it change the way you pray and the way you see your children. And as you do, remember that God is watching over His Word to perform it. "Then the Lord said to me, 'You have seen well, for I am watching over My word to perform it'" (Jeremiah 1:12, ESV).

This journey is one of love, faith, and hope. You are not alone. You have the promises of God, the power of the Holy Spirit, and the authority of Jesus Christ backing every word you speak. Now, let's begin.

Chapter 1

Power of Words in a Parent's Mouth

Words are never just words. They are carriers of meaning, emotion, intention, and power. In the natural world, words are how we communicate; in the spiritual realm, words are how we create, shape, and release authority. From the very beginning, God demonstrated the power of spoken words. "Then God said, 'Let there be light'; and there was light" (Genesis 1:3, NKJV). God did not wave His hand, nor did He form the universe with a gesture—He spoke. And when He spoke, things happened. His words formed the heavens, separated the land from the sea, called forth living creatures, and shaped mankind in His image. This divine pattern should cause every parent to pause and consider the tremendous power placed in their mouth. If God created with words, what are we creating with ours?

Our children are constantly listening. Whether they show it or not, they are absorbing the atmosphere we create with our words. Every word spoken in the home builds or breaks something inside of them. Encouragement builds identity. Criticism cuts it down. Affirmation fosters courage. Fearful speech feeds anxiety. Silence can sometimes even speak louder than sound. But when our words align with God's Word, something supernatural begins to happen in our children's lives. We begin to shape them not according to our moods or emotions but according to the design of the One who made them.

Proverbs 18:21 declares, "Death and life are in the power of the tongue, and those who love it will eat its fruit" (NKJV). This verse isn't a poetic metaphor—it's a spiritual reality. Our tongues hold the power to bring life or death to situations, relationships, and especially our children's development. This power was entrusted to us by God, not for manipulation or condemnation, but for blessing. A parent's words become the internal soundtrack of a child's future. Children often grow up repeating things they heard over and over in their childhood—either words that built them up or words that tore them down. What we repeatedly say to our children becomes a script they carry into adulthood.

Scripture constantly draws attention to the weight of words. Jesus Himself warned, "For by your words you will be justified, and by your words you will be condemned" (Matthew 12:37, NKJV). This is not just a warning of judgment; it's an invitation to recognize how seriously God takes speech. The tongue is not neutral. It either partners with God's purposes or contradicts them. James, the brother of Jesus, offered a vivid metaphor: "Even so the tongue is a little member and boasts great things. See how great a forest a little fire kindles!" (James 3:5, NKJV). He continues by describing how a single spark from the tongue can ignite destruction. If that's true in the negative, the opposite is also true—our words can ignite healing, purpose, and hope.

As parents, we are not merely caregivers—we are spiritual architects. Every word of blessing or faith that we speak is like a brick laid on the foundation of our children's identity. God has given us divine authority to partner with His Spirit and speak life into our homes. That authority must be used with reverence. We cannot afford to speak casually about our children's futures. Saying things like "He'll never learn" or "She's just difficult" might seem harmless at the moment, but these words lodge into the heart. When children hear negative speech about themselves repeatedly, it becomes a kind of prophecy they unconsciously fulfill.

On the other hand, when we speak Scripture over them, we are sowing seeds of truth that God Himself will water. Isaiah 55:11 offers this promise: "So shall My word be that goes forth from My mouth; it shall not return to Me void, but it shall accomplish what I please, and it shall prosper in the thing for which I sent it" (NKJV). When a parent declares God's promises, those words take on the power of divine assignment. They go out with a mission, they don't come back empty, and they work in ways we cannot see.

Even when children rebel or wander, the words of faith we have spoken over them are not lost. God remembers every declaration made in agreement with His Word. The prodigal son may have run far from home, but the identity his father spoke over him—"my son"—was never removed. And when he returned, the father's words were waiting: "For this my son was dead and is alive again; he was lost and is found" (Luke 15:24, NKJV). The power of a parent's voice of love and truth can draw a child back from any distance. Never underestimate the long reach of words spoken in faith.

The enemy understands the power of words, which is why he works so hard to distort them in the home. He stirs up anger, offense, impatience, and fear, hoping parents will lash out and wound with their tongues. But when we are mindful of our speech and filled with the Holy Spirit, we can resist that trap. The Bible gives us clear instruction: "Let no corrupt word proceed out of your mouth, but what is good for necessary edification, that it may impart grace to the hearers" (Ephesians 4:29, NKJV). The goal is not perfection but edification—building up, not tearing down.

There is a generational impact on our words as well. God told the people of Israel to be intentional about how they used their words with their children. "And these words which I command you today shall be in your heart. You shall teach them diligently to your children..." (Deuteronomy 6:6–7, NKJV). God didn't suggest this as a religious formality; He commanded it as a way to shape entire families for generations. Speaking the Word of God in the home trains the mind, reinforces the spirit, and places a child's feet on a firm foundation.

Some parents hesitate to speak Scripture aloud because it feels unnatural or awkward. But speaking God's Word doesn't have to sound like preaching—it can be woven naturally into conversation. Instead of saying, "I hope things work out for you," try saying, "God has a good plan for your life" (Jeremiah 29:11, NKJV). When your child feels anxious, declare, "God has not given you a spirit of fear, but of power and of love and of a sound mind" (2 Timothy 1:7, NKJV). These phrases become more than good advice—they are declarations of truth that push back spiritual darkness.

There is also healing in our words. Proverbs 12:18 says, "There is one who speaks like the piercings of a sword, but the tongue of the wise promotes health" (NKJV). This verse reveals a powerful secret: wise words can actually bring emotional and spiritual healing. Many children are carrying invisible wounds—words they've heard from peers, teachers, or even family members. But when a parent begins to speak God's truth into those places, healing begins. A simple phrase like "You are deeply loved by God and by me" can become a balm to a wounded soul.

We must also remember the way Jesus spoke. He never spoke carelessly. His words were spirit and life. He said, "The words that I speak to you are spirit, and they are life" (John 6:63, NKJV). As followers of Christ, we are called to reflect that same life-giving speech. Every day, we are faced with the choice: will my words today give life, or will they harm? Will they point my child toward God's truth or feed the confusion of the world?

Even correction should be guided by love and truth. Discipline is necessary, but it must never be void of grace. Hebrews 12:10 reminds us that God disciplines us "for our profit, that we may be partakers of His holiness" (NKJV). His discipline is purposeful and never mean-spirited - so too, when we correct our children, it should be with an aim to guide, not shame. The way we speak, even in moments of discipline, will either help our children understand their value or cause them to question it.

There is a beautiful example in Scripture of how God speaks over His children. When Jesus was baptized, the heavens opened, and a voice declared, "This is My beloved Son, in whom I am well pleased" (Matthew 3:17, NKJV). That moment did not occur after Jesus performed miracles or completed His mission. It came at the beginning of His ministry. God publicly affirmed His Son's identity and value simply because He was His. What if every child could hear their parent speak words like these over them: "You are mine. I love you. I'm proud of you, not because of what you do, but because of who you are."

As parents, we also have the power to shape destiny through prayerful declarations. Hannah, the mother of Samuel, prayed with such faith and surrender that her son was marked for prophetic destiny even before he was born. After she dedicated him to the Lord, she declared, "My heart rejoices in the Lord... The Lord makes poor and makes rich; He brings low and lifts up" (1 Samuel 2:1,7, NKJV). Her words reflected deep faith and trust in God's sovereignty. Samuel would go on to become one of the greatest prophets in Israel's history. Could it be that her prayers and declarations helped prepare the way?

Your children may not remember every lecture or lesson, but they will remember the words that consistently came from your mouth. They will carry them into classrooms, relationships, and adulthood. One day, they may even speak those same words over their own children. Let's make sure the words we speak are worth repeating. Let's ensure they are filled with truth, hope, and the promises of God.

We are not left to our own strength in this task. The Holy Spirit is our helper. He can remind us, prompt us, and even give us the right words to speak at the right time. "But the Helper, the Holy Spirit, whom the Father will send in My name, He will teach you all things, and bring to your remembrance all things that I said to you" (John 14:26, NKJV). As we walk closely with God, our mouths will be filled with His wisdom, and our homes will reflect His heart.

The words of a parent are powerful, not because of volume or vocabulary, but because of position. God has placed you in a unique role of influence and authority. Your words carry weight in your child's heart and spirit. Let them be words of blessing, life, and promise. Let them be echoes of the Word of God, shaping your children for a future filled with purpose.

Chapter 2

Praying with Confidence, God's Word is His Will

Prayer is not merely a spiritual habit or a religious tradition—it is a divine invitation to partner with God in the unfolding of His will. When a parent prays for their child, heaven pays attention. God designed prayer as a sacred channel through which His power and promises are brought to bear upon the earth. Yet many parents struggle with confidence in their prayers. They wonder, *Am I saying the right things? Is God really listening? Will my prayers make a difference?* These are common questions, but they miss one essential truth: when we pray God's Word, we are praying His will, and there is no greater confidence than knowing we are praying in perfect alignment with the heart of God.

The apostle John gives us this assurance: "Now this is the confidence that we have in Him, that if we ask anything according to His will, He hears us. And if we know that He hears us, whatever we ask, we know that we have the petitions that we have asked of Him" (1 John 5:14–15, NKJV). These words should quiet every doubt and stir fresh faith in every parent's heart. God's will is not hidden from us. It has been revealed in His Word. Every time we take a Scripture promise and speak it over our children in prayer, we are aligning our words with the unchanging purposes of heaven.

God never intended for prayer to be guesswork. He never asked us to approach Him uncertainly or timidly. Hebrews 4:16 urges us to "come boldly to the throne of grace, that we may obtain mercy and find grace to help in time of need" (NKJV). Boldness in prayer is not arrogance—it is trust in the character of the One we're speaking to. It is the confidence that we are welcome, that we are heard, and that we are praying not our own ideas but His own will, expressed through His Word.

The Bible is filled with the revealed will of God. His promises are not vague expressions of goodwill—they are legal declarations of His intentions toward us and our children. When God says, "I will instruct you and teach you in the way you should go; I will guide you with My eye" (Psalm 32:8, NKJV), He is not offering a mere suggestion. He is making a commitment. When He says, "All your children shall be taught by the Lord, and great shall be the peace of your children" (Isaiah 54:13, NKJV), He is revealing a specific part of His will for our families. As parents, we do not have to come up with our own language in prayer—we can borrow His. We can take these promises and turn them into prayers of faith.

Jesus modeled this kind of prayer when He walked the earth. He constantly referenced Scripture in His teaching, His decisions, and His prayers. He prayed in agreement with the Father and submitted completely to His will. In the Garden of Gethsemane, as He prepared to face the cross, He said, "Not My will, but Yours, be done" (Luke 22:42, NKJV). This complete surrender did not weaken His prayers—it empowered them. The same is true for us. Praying God's Word is not about getting our way; it's about declaring *His* way and trusting Him to work it out in His perfect timing.

Parents who pray the Word of God over their children are not simply reacting to circumstances—they are planting seeds of divine purpose. God watches over His Word, not just our emotions. "Then the Lord said to me, 'You have seen well, for I am watching over My word to perform it'" (Jeremiah 1:12, ESV). This means our most effective prayers are those rooted in Scripture. When we pray, "Lord, let my child walk in Your truth," we are echoing 3 John 1:4, which says, "I have no greater joy than to hear that my children walk in truth" (NKJV). That echo reaches heaven with clarity and power because it originates in His Word.

It is not uncommon for parents to feel overwhelmed, especially when their children face challenges—spiritual battles, emotional struggles, or worldly influences that seem too strong. But in those moments, we are not helpless. God has given us the sword of the Spirit, which is "the word of God" (Ephesians 6:17, NKJV). Our prayers can be more than heartfelt pleas; they can be strategic, Word-filled declarations that strike down the lies of the enemy. When a child is battling fear, we can pray, "God has not given my child a spirit of fear, but of power and of love and of a sound mind" (2 Timothy 1:7, NKJV). When they are unsure of their identity, we can declare, "My child is fearfully and wonderfully made" (Psalm 139:14, NKJV). When they are tempted, we can claim, "No temptation has overtaken them except such as is common to man; but God is faithful, who will not allow them to be tempted beyond what they are able" (1 Corinthians 10:13, NKJV). Each prayer becomes a spiritual weapon.

Confidence in prayer grows as we begin to see God's faithfulness. He is not slow to hear, nor is He distant. "The Lord is near to all who call upon Him, to all who call upon Him in truth" (Psalm 145:18, NKJV). When our children are far from us—whether at school, away at college, or making choices that grieve us—God is still near to them, and He hears us. He is the same God who heard Hagar cry out in the wilderness and who heard the groaning of the Israelites in Egypt. He hears parents who cry out in the night for their children. He hears the whispered prayers said over a sleeping baby, the desperate prayers cried into a pillow, and the joyful declarations shouted in faith.

One of the greatest examples of praying God's Word is found in the life of Daniel. In Daniel 9, he reads the writings of the prophet Jeremiah and sees the promise of Israel's return from captivity. He doesn't just celebrate it; he begins to pray it. He aligns himself with what God already said and brings it before the throne in fasting and intercession. That is our model. We search the Scriptures for the promises God has made to us and our children, and then we pray them back to Him—not to remind Him, but to engage in covenant partnership. God's promises are not magic formulas, but they are reliable foundations. He never breaks His Word.

It's also important to remember that our prayers, when based on His Word, are not limited by time. They extend beyond the moment. Isaiah 59:21 offers a remarkable promise: "As for Me," says the Lord, "this is My covenant with them: My Spirit who is upon you, and My words which I have put in your mouth, shall not depart from your mouth, nor from the mouth of your descendants... from this time and forevermore" (NKJV). This reveals a generational promise. When we speak and pray the Word, it doesn't just bless the moment—it sets a spiritual legacy in motion. Prayers prayed today will echo through the lives of our children and even their children.

We must also trust the process. Sometimes, we expect immediate results, and when we don't see them, we question if our prayers are working. But Jesus taught that the kingdom of God is like a seed. "First the blade, then the head, after that the full grain in the head" (Mark 4:28, NKJV). This means that our prayers often take time to manifest. The answer may not appear overnight, but the seed is growing beneath the surface. Faith says, "Even when I don't see it yet, I know God is working." When we pray the Word, we can trust that the seed is good and the harvest will come.

Our confidence in prayer should not be tied to our feelings. Some days, we feel strong in faith, and other days, we feel weak. But God's Word does not change. His promises remain true regardless of our emotional state. That's why it's so important to build our prayers on His Word and not on our circumstances. The psalmist declared, "Forever, O Lord, Your word is settled in heaven" (Psalm 119:89, NKJV). When we pray what is settled in heaven, we bring that settled truth into the unsettled places of our children's lives.

We are also invited to ask with boldness and persistence. Jesus taught about the persistent widow who kept coming to the judge, and He said, "Shall God not avenge His own elect who cry out day and night to Him?" (Luke 18:7, NKJV). This is not a story about wearing God down—it's a story about unwavering faith. When we pray consistently, even through delay or difficulty, we are expressing trust that God is faithful to His Word.

There is tremendous peace that comes from praying with confidence. The apostle Paul wrote, "Be anxious for nothing, but in everything by prayer and supplication, with thanksgiving, let your requests be made known to God; and the peace of God... will guard your hearts and minds through Christ Jesus" (Philippians 4:6–7, NKJV). That peace is not based on the outcome—it's based on the confidence that God has heard and He is working. Prayer may not always change our circumstances immediately, but it will change us. It will anchor our hearts in God's faithfulness and silence the voice of fear.

In the end, praying God's Word over our children is one of the most powerful, consistent, and holy things we can do. We are not casting words into the wind—we are sending arrows into battle. We are not begging—we are partnering. We are not wondering—we are standing on promises that cannot fail. The more we know God's Word, the more boldly we will pray. The more boldly we pray, the more peace we will experience. And the more peace we walk in, the more our homes will reflect the presence of the One whose Word never returns void.

Chapter 3
Faith Comes by Hearing

Faith is not a feeling, nor is it something we inherit genetically. It is spiritual, alive, and dynamic. It grows, develops, and takes root.

And most importantly, it comes by hearing. Not hearing just anything, but specifically hearing the Word of God. Scripture makes this truth unshakably clear: "So then faith comes by hearing and hearing by the word of God" (Romans 10:17, NKJV). This verse is not simply a truth for adults or ministers—it is a principle for all people, including the smallest of children. God designed the human heart to respond to His Word. That is how He reaches us, grows us, and matures our trust in Him. If you want faith to rise in your home, then your home must be filled with the sound of God's Word.

Children are shaped by what they hear—constantly and repeatedly. Their worldview, self-image, and confidence are all directly impacted by the voices around them. A child's heart is like rich soil, and words are like seeds. The more they hear the truth of Scripture, the more those seeds take root and bear the fruit of faith. This is not wishful thinking. It's divine design. When God told the Israelites how to raise their children, He didn't emphasize ceremonies or traditions first—He emphasized His words. "And these words which I command you today shall be in your heart. You shall teach them diligently to your children" (Deuteronomy 6:6–7, NKJV). Why? Because when the Word is heard consistently, faith becomes natural.

Faith does not develop in silence. It needs a voice. That voice must speak the truth, not just concepts or good morals, but actual Scripture— words that came from the mouth of God. Even before children understand all the meanings behind the verses, their spirits recognize the source. The Word of God is living. It carries spiritual weight. Hebrews 4:12 says, "For the word of God is living and powerful, and sharper than any two-edged sword" (NKJV). When that living Word enters the hearing of a child, it begins a process that no human can fully comprehend or replicate.

The same is true for parents. We cannot expect to walk in strong faith for our children if our own hearts are not being nourished by the Word. If our ears are full of fear, media noise, and worry, then our prayers and our perspectives will suffer. But when we feed our minds and hearts with Scripture, faith rises. Hearing the Word is not a one-time experience; it must become a way of life. Just as food nourishes the body, God's Word sustains the spirit. And a faith-filled parent becomes a powerful voice in a child's life.

We live in a noisy world. Voices are competing for the attention of our children. The culture is loud, the internet is loud, and the entertainment industry is loud. And often, those voices are not only godless—they are anti-God. They challenge truth, distort identity, and erode moral foundations. If we do not intentionally raise the volume of God's Word in our homes, we are unintentionally allowing other voices to fill the silence. Silence is not neutral. Where God's Word is not heard, confusion takes its place. But where it is consistently spoken and honored, clarity, faith, and peace follow.

One of the clearest examples of this is seen in the life of Timothy. Paul reminded him of the spiritual foundation that had been laid in him since childhood. He wrote, "From childhood you have known the Holy Scriptures, which are able to make you wise for salvation through faith which is in Christ Jesus" (2 Timothy 3:15, NKJV). How did Timothy come to know the Scriptures from childhood? Through his mother and grandmother. Paul even names them—Lois and Eunice—as women of sincere faith who passed that faith on through teaching and example. Their words, rooted in Scripture, built a legacy of faith that made Timothy a strong leader in the early church.

This is the kind of generational impact God desires for every family. When Scripture becomes a natural part of a home's rhythm—

read at the table, spoken at bedtime, sung in songs, referenced in decision-making—it forms a pattern that the heart embraces. Children learn to value what their parents value. If they see us turning to God's Word in times of need, they will do the same. If they hear us quote Scripture instead of panic, they will follow suit. Faith is contagious. And nothing spreads faith like the Word of God spoken with sincerity.

It's important to remember that hearing does not only happen during structured Bible times. Faith can grow through spontaneous, spirit-led moments. A verse whispered during a tearful conversation. A Scripture referenced while riding in the car. A bedtime story that includes God's promises. These moments may seem small, but they carry eternal weight. God multiplies our efforts when we sow His Word in love. He promised, "My word... shall not return to Me void, but it shall accomplish what I please" (Isaiah 55:11, NKJV). That means every time you speak Scripture over your child, something is happening—even if you don't see it yet.

This truth is especially important for parents who are believing for children who are struggling. If your child is wrestling with doubt, rebellion, addiction, anxiety, or other battles, the answer is not to pull back but to press in. Keep speaking the Word. Keep creating an atmosphere where Scripture is present, even if it seems to be resisted. The seed still works. The soil may look dry, but the seed is alive. God is not asking you to fix everything—He's asking you to trust His Word to do what only it can do.

There's another layer to this truth that's vital for parents: the way *we* hear determines the strength of our faith as much as it does for our children. Adults can fall into the trap of becoming familiar with Scripture to the point of no longer listening. We assume we know it, and in doing so, we stop hearing. But faith does not come from having heard—it comes from hearing. Present tense. It's a daily choice to turn our ears toward the voice of God and let His truth shape our mindset. The more you hear His Word, the stronger your faith becomes—and your children will notice the difference.

Faith is not taught only in lessons; it is taught in the way we live. When children hear parents speak confidently, pray boldly, and worship sincerely, they are learning more than words—they are learning trust. When they hear us confess promises rather than complaints, declare healing instead of hopelessness, and speak the truth when others doubt, they are witnessing what living faith looks like. The sound of Scripture should not only be found in devotion time—it should echo through daily life.

Psalm 78 gives us a powerful vision of generational faith through the Word. It says, "We will not hide them from their children, telling to the generation to come the praises of the Lord, and His strength and His wonderful works that He has done… That the generation to come might know them… and declare them to their children" (Psalm 78:4,6, NKJV). This is a picture of intentional storytelling, teaching, and repetition. The truth of God is passed down when it is spoken aloud, celebrated, and remembered. It cannot be hidden in silence. If we do not tell them, someone else will.

Jesus understood the power of hearing. He constantly said, "He who has ears to hear, let him hear!" (Matthew 11:15, NKJV). He knew that hearing with the heart was the gateway to transformation. That's why Satan works hard to distract, distort, and dull our spiritual ears. He knows that if we truly *hear* God's Word, faith will rise and defeat his lies. As parents, our job is to tune the frequency of our homes to God's voice so that faith has room to grow.

It is also important to recognize the role of worship and music in building faith. Songs filled with Scripture help children (and adults) internalize truth without even realizing it. A child may not be ready to memorize a full Bible verse, but they can sing a chorus that's rooted in Scripture, and that melody will carry the truth deep into their soul. God wired us to respond to rhythm and melody—it's no accident that the largest book in the Bible, Psalms, is a book of songs. Faith grows through hearing the Word in many forms.

Sometimes, we make faith too complicated. We try to muster it up emotionally or achieve it through effort. But Scripture says that it comes simply by hearing God's Word. Our job is not to create faith—it's to create an environment where faith can be heard. And the more often our children hear God's truth, the more their hearts will be conditioned to believe it. Even when they face trials, even when the world challenges what they've learned, the Word inside them will speak louder.

One day, your child will face something difficult—peer pressure, failure, heartbreak, or spiritual confusion. At that moment, they may not remember every Sunday School lesson, but they will remember what they consistently heard at home. Was it Scripture? Was it faith? Was it hope? Or was it fear, anxiety, and silence? We are writing their internal playlist with our words. Let's make sure it is filled with faith-producing truth.

We are promised in Romans 10:8, "The word is near you, in your mouth and in your heart" (NKJV). This shows us a powerful sequence— what we hear, we believe, and what we believe, we begin to speak. The same is true for our children. As they hear us speak God's Word, it becomes near to them. It gets in their mouth, then in their heart, and eventually comes out in their prayers, songs, and conversations. That is when you begin to see the fruit of what you've sown.

Do not underestimate what is happening when your child hears you speak God's promises over them. You may be speaking into the future. You may be watering seeds that will bloom at just the right moment. You may be equipping them for a battle you won't even see. But God sees. And He honors every word of faith spoken in love. He is faithful to complete what He starts, and He has started something beautiful in your family through His Word.

Let your home be a house where Scripture is honored, heard, and celebrated. Let your voice be one that speaks truth, love, and faith—not just to correct behavior but to build belief. And let your own heart be continually filled with God's Word so that what flows from your mouth carries the power to produce faith in every listener—especially the ones growing up under your care.

Chapter 4
Your House—The Generational Impact of Faith

Faith is not a solitary journey. Though it is personal, it is never meant to be private or contained within a single life. From the beginning, God's design has always been generational. He blesses, He calls, and He covenants with families. When one person in a household chooses to believe, that decision ripples through time, reaching children, grandchildren, and generations yet unborn. What we do with our faith today directly impacts our families tomorrow. This is both a powerful promise and a sobering responsibility.

God's covenant with Abraham makes this truth undeniable. Abraham didn't just receive a personal blessing—he received a generational one. God said, "In you all the families of the earth shall be blessed" (Genesis 12:3, NKJV), and later, "And I will establish My covenant between Me and you and your descendants after you in their generations" (Genesis 17:7, NKJV). Abraham's faith didn't die with him. It marked Isaac. It influenced Jacob. It birthed a nation. One man's decision to trust God became the foundation for Israel's entire relationship with the Lord. That is the impact of faith lived out in obedience.

This pattern continues throughout Scripture. God speaks not only to individuals but to households. When the children of Israel were about to be delivered from Egypt, God gave instructions for the Passover: each *household* was to be covered by the blood of a lamb. Exodus 12:3 says, "Every man shall take for himself a lamb, according to the house of his father, a lamb for a household." And verse 13 follows, "When I see the blood, I will pass over you" (NKJV). That was a house-wide covering, not an individual one. It teaches us that the choices we make in faith affect everyone under our roof.

Centuries later, when Joshua stood on the edge of the Promised Land, he declared his loyalty with boldness: "As for me and my house, we will serve the Lord" (Joshua 24:15, NKJV). He didn't just speak for himself—he spoke for his entire family. That statement was not controlling; it was covenantal. He understood that his leadership as a man of faith would shape the spiritual direction of his household. He knew that his worship, obedience, and reverence would echo in the lives of those who followed after him.

In the New Testament, this same truth continues. When the Philippian jailer asked Paul and Silas what he must do to be saved, their answer was profound: "Believe on the Lord Jesus Christ, and you will be saved, you and your household" (Acts 16:31, NKJV). The promise was immediate, but it wasn't isolated. The jailer's response to the gospel would open a door of salvation to his entire family. And Scripture confirms, "Then immediately he and all his family were baptized" (Acts 16:33, NKJV). This is God's heart. He doesn't just want individuals; He wants generations.

Your faith is not just about you—it's about your house. It's about your children, their children, and even the great-grandchildren you may never meet. When you believe God's promises, pray His Word, and live by His Spirit, you are building a spiritual foundation that others will stand on. You are planting trees whose shade you may never sit under. But God sees. And He honors generational faith.

The enemy understands the generational nature of God's blessing, which is why he works so hard to sever faith from the family line. He wants to disrupt the transfer of truth, silence the voices of prayer, and replace legacies of righteousness with cycles of brokenness. But when one person in a family says, "Enough," and stands in faith, the cycle can be broken. What was passed down in sin can be stopped, and what begins in faith can be passed on in righteousness.

Psalm 103:17 says, "But the mercy of the Lord is from everlasting to everlasting on those who fear Him, and His righteousness to children's children" (NKJV). This is not a poetic ideal—it is a promise. God's mercy and righteousness extend far beyond the moment. They reach into the lineage of those who love Him. That means every prayer, every Scripture spoken, and every moment of obedience you walk in today is building something your children's children will benefit from tomorrow.

Consider Timothy again, the young pastor Paul mentored. Paul wrote, "I call to remembrance the genuine faith that is in you, which dwelt first in your grandmother Lois and your mother Eunice, and I am persuaded is in you also" (2 Timothy 1:5, NKJV). Notice the order: grandmother, mother, then Timothy. Three generations of faith, passed down not by religious duty but by sincere, lived-out belief. That's what real legacy looks like—not perfect families, but families where faith is real, consistent, and visible.

Even David, the man after God's own heart, left a legacy through his faith and worship. Though his life included many failures, his heart for God was undeniable, and it influenced his son Solomon. When Solomon dedicated the temple, he referred to the God of his father, David, and prayed that God would fulfill the promises made to his father. And God did. Because faith, even flawed and imperfect, leaves an imprint when it is genuine.

Some parents feel discouraged because their children are not currently walking with the Lord. But faith is not measured only by present behavior—it is measured by eternal promise. God is not finished. What you've spoken, prayed, and lived in faith is still working. Isaiah 59:21 offers a declaration worth holding onto: "My Spirit who is upon you, and My words which I have put in your mouth, shall not depart from your mouth... nor from the mouth of your descendants... from this time and forevermore" (NKJV). The Word you've sown is active. The Spirit who empowers you is still reaching. God's generational plan is in motion.

The way we walk out our faith in front of our children matters. If we treat the church as optional, they will, too. If we minimize prayer and the Word, they will learn to do the same. But when they see us worship when we're weary, speak Scripture when we're unsure, and love people even when it's hard, they begin to understand that faith is not a religion—it's a relationship. And that relationship is worth building a life upon.

Our homes are meant to be centers of spiritual legacy. That doesn't mean they are free from trouble, but it means they are anchored in truth. The enemy will attack, culture will shift, and challenges will come— but the foundation of faith laid in a household can withstand the storm. Jesus taught this in Matthew 7 when He said, "Whoever hears these sayings of Mine, and does them, I will liken him to a wise man who built his house on the rock... and it did not fall, for it was founded on the rock" (Matthew 7:24–25, NKJV). Your obedience becomes your children's stability. Your faith becomes their inheritance.

Sometimes, we think of inheritance only in terms of money or material blessings. But the most powerful inheritance you can leave your children is a knowledge of God, a history of answered prayers, and a household shaped by the Word. Proverbs 13:22 reminds us, "A good man leaves an inheritance to his children's children" (NKJV). That inheritance includes more than wealth. It includes wisdom, faith, character, and legacy.

When you gather your children to pray, you are passing down more than words—you are modeling trust. When you read Scripture at the dinner table or share a testimony of God's provision, you are building a memory that may later become a lifeline. When you admit failure and ask forgiveness in front of your family, you are teaching humility and grace. These moments become part of the spiritual DNA of your house.

Even the smallest acts of obedience matter. The times you take your children to church even when it's inconvenient, the songs of worship you sing in the kitchen, the Scripture verses taped to the bathroom mirror—these are the things that build faith over time. Deuteronomy 11:19 instructs us, "You shall teach them [God's words] to your children, speaking of them when you sit in your house, when you walk by the way, when you lie down, and when you rise up" (NKJV). This kind of consistent, intentional faith creates a spiritual rhythm that shapes the heart.

There is also power in blessing. Throughout Scripture, fathers and mothers blessed their children with words spoken in faith. Isaac blessed Jacob. Jacob blessed his sons. Even Jesus, when surrounded by children, laid hands on them and blessed them. These blessings were more than kind words—they were prophetic declarations spoken under the inspiration of the Spirit. We have that same authority. Speak life over your children. Declare God's promises over them. Speak as one who believes the future is full of God's goodness.

If you come from a family that lacked this kind of spiritual heritage, take heart. You can be the one to begin it. God often starts new stories in unexpected places. You may not have inherited faith from your parents, but your children can inherit it from you. The line of blessing can begin with your surrender. The river of legacy can begin with your yes to God. Psalm 145:4 says, "One generation shall praise Your works to another, and shall declare Your mighty acts" (NKJV). You can be the voice that declares, the hand that sows, and the heart that believes for the generations to come.

You and your house matter to God. Your family is not forgotten. Your prayers are not in vain. Your obedience is not wasted. Every time you choose to believe, to trust, and to live by the Word, you are building something eternal. And God, who is faithful to a thousand generations, is watching over His promise.

Chapter 5
God's Covenant with Families

God is a covenant-making God. From the opening chapters of the Bible to its final promises, the theme of covenant runs like a golden thread, revealing God's commitment, consistency, and unfailing love. However, God's covenants were never intended solely for individuals—they have always encompassed families. From Noah to Abraham, from David to the new covenant in Christ, we see again and again that God's heart beats for the family unit. His blessings extend not only to the one who believes but also to their children and their children's children. This truth brings both comfort and challenge. It means that when a parent enters into a covenant relationship with God, the effects are passed down through generations. The implications of that covenant reach far beyond one life.

In Genesis 6, God looked upon a corrupt and violent world and chose one man—Noah. But God didn't just save Noah alone. Genesis 6:18 (NKJV) says, "But I will establish My covenant with you, and you shall go into the ark—you, your sons, your wife, and your sons' wives with you." From the very first major covenant in Scripture, we see that God includes the family. He could have chosen to spare Noah and start over, but instead, He extended that mercy and protection to his entire household. This was not a coincidence. It was a pattern. The covenant relationship established with Noah brought salvation to his whole family. That same covenant preserved humanity and reset the course of history.

A few chapters later, God enters into another covenant—this time with Abram, later named Abraham. In Genesis 17:7 (NKJV), God declares, "And I will establish My covenant between Me and you and your descendants after you in their generations, for an everlasting covenant, to be God to you and your descendants after you." Here, the generational scope of God's covenant is unmistakable. It is not temporary. It is not limited. It is everlasting. God promises not just to bless Abraham but to be God to his descendants. This single covenant became the foundation for the entire nation of Israel. And it began with one man's willingness to believe and obey.

Abraham's faithfulness had a profound impact on his son Isaac. Genesis 26:24 (NKJV) records God speaking to Isaac and saying, "I am the God of your father Abraham; do not fear, for I am with you. I will bless you and multiply your descendants for My servant Abraham's sake." Isaac received promises not just because of his actions but because of the covenant God had made with his father. That is the power of generational covenant. It places a covering over our children that goes beyond our lifetimes. God honors the faith of parents and grandparents and continues to move on behalf of the family line.

When we understand that God deals with families covenantally, it changes the way we pray, the way we parent, and the way we see our future. Our role is not simply to raise good children—it is to raise covenant children. Children who grow up aware of God's promises, covered by God's Word, and marked by a spiritual inheritance. Psalm 112:1–2 (NKJV) says, "Blessed is the man who fears the Lord... His descendants will be mighty on earth; the generation of the upright will be blessed." God's favor does not stop with us—it moves through us and flows into our children.

The covenant God made with David echoes this again. David had a heart after God, and his desire to build a house for the Lord led to God making a powerful promise: "When your days are fulfilled, and you rest with your fathers, I will set up your seed after you... and I will establish his kingdom. He shall build a house for My name, and I will establish the throne of his kingdom forever" (2 Samuel 7:12–13 NKJV). David's covenant with God impacted Solomon, and even beyond Solomon, it pointed to Jesus—the Son of David whose kingdom will never end. Once again, we see that God's covenant extends beyond the lifespan of one person. It shapes the course of generations.

For Christian parents today, we are invited into the most powerful covenant of all—the new covenant through Jesus Christ. Hebrews 8:6 tells us, "But now He has obtained a more excellent ministry, inasmuch as He is also Mediator of a better covenant, which was established on better promises." This covenant is sealed not with the blood of bulls or goats but with the blood of the Lamb. And this better covenant comes with better promises, including the promise of salvation for our entire households. Acts 2:39 (NKJV) declares, "For the promise is to you and your children, and to all who are afar off, as many as the Lord our God will call."

The new covenant does not cancel the principle of family covenant—it fulfills and expands it. Through Christ, we are adopted into God's family, and our children are included in that invitation. God still deals with households. He still responds to parents who cry out for their children. He still honors prayers that are built on covenant promises. When you stand in faith for your child's salvation, healing, protection, or destiny, you are not begging an indifferent deity—you are standing on the legal foundation of a blood-bought covenant.

This means we can pray with boldness. We can claim God's promises not only for ourselves but for our families. We can declare, "As for me and my house, we will serve the Lord" (Joshua 24:15 NKJV) with the full assurance that God is faithful to keep His Word. We can pray, "Lord, fulfill Your covenant in my child's life. Let them know You. Let them walk in Your ways. Let the destiny You wrote for them come to pass." These are not selfish prayers; they are covenant prayers. They are grounded in the very heart of God.

Covenant also brings with it responsibility. It's not a one-sided relationship. God makes promises, but He also calls us to walk in obedience. Deuteronomy 6:6–7 (NKJV) gives parents this charge: "And these words which I command you today shall be in your heart. You shall teach them diligently to your children." Covenant parents are called to be covenant teachers. We must be faithful to pass on the truths of God, to model His character, and to train our children in

29

righteousness. We are not merely raising good citizens—we are raising sons and daughters of the King.

This doesn't mean we will do everything perfectly. But even in our weakness, God remains faithful. Our imperfection does not break the covenant. His grace upholds it. He knows our frame, and He is full of mercy. Psalm 103:17–18 (NKJV) reminds us, "But the mercy of the Lord is from everlasting to everlasting on those who fear Him, and His righteousness to children's children, to such as keep His covenant, and to those who remember His commandments to do them." God is patient with families. He gives us time. He gives us grace. He gives us the Holy Spirit to guide us.

For families who feel broken or fragmented, the promise of a covenant remains strong. God does not reject you because of divorce, dysfunction, or past mistakes. His covenant is not based on our perfection—it is rooted in His love. Joel 2:25 (NKJV) says, "So I will restore to you the years that the swarming locust has eaten." God is a restorer. He can restore families. He can bring wayward children home. He can take fractured homes and make them whole again. His covenant includes healing, reconciliation, and hope.

One of the most powerful moments in Scripture is found in Malachi 4:6 (NKJV), the very last verse of the Old Testament: "And he will turn the hearts of the fathers to the children, and the hearts of the children to their fathers." This is the fruit of the covenant—the restoration of relationships between generations. It is not just about rules and blessings. It's about hearts being turned, connected, and healed. That is what God longs to do in every family.

In your own home, you can begin to live as a covenant family. Speak the promises of God aloud. Bless your children in the name of Jesus. Establish a rhythm of Scripture and prayer. Celebrate God's goodness together. Invite His presence into your daily life. These habits may seem small, but they are covenant actions. They signal to heaven that your family is aligned with God's purposes. They build a spiritual inheritance that will bless generations.

Never forget that God is more invested in your family than you are. He created it. He designed the generational structure. He authored the idea of legacy. And He has made promises to cover your family in every season. Whether your children are babies, teenagers, or adults, whether your household is united or divided, whether your past is full of faith or full of mistakes—God's covenant still stands. And He is faithful to complete what He began.

Chapter 6
Building a Prayer Ark for Your Children

In times of increasing darkness and cultural decline, the call to protect and prepare our children becomes more urgent than ever. The world is not a neutral place—it is a battleground for the hearts and minds of the next generation. The values of faith, righteousness, and truth are under assault on every front. But God has given us a model for how to respond. In the days of Noah, when the earth was filled with corruption and violence, God called one man to build an ark—not just for himself, but for his family. Hebrews 11:7 (NKJV) tells us, "By faith Noah, being divinely warned of things not yet seen, moved with godly fear, prepared an ark for the saving of his household." That verse speaks to every believing parent today. We are called to build spiritual arks for our children—places of safety, instruction, and covenant that will preserve them in the storms of the world.

Noah's Ark was not built overnight. It was not convenient. It was not popular. But it was essential. And it was built by faith. Noah believed God's warning before there were clouds in the sky. He obeyed instructions that seemed ridiculous to the people around him. And he did it all with his family in mind. This kind of faith is not passive—it is active, deliberate, and sacrificial. It labors not for personal comfort but for generational survival. Building an ark means creating a culture in your home where God's Word is honored, His voice is heard, and His presence is welcomed. It means intentionally preparing your children for what's ahead, not just reacting to what's happening now.

An ark is a structure of preservation. Spiritually speaking, we build it with truth. The wood and nails of Noah's Ark are like the Scriptures and prayers we use today. Every Bible verse spoken over a child is a plank in that ark. Every time we pray for protection, speak identity, or teach them to trust God, we're adding a beam to the structure that will carry them. The world outside may rage, but the child who has been taught to hear the Shepherd's voice will remain steady. They will face storms, yes, but they will not be overwhelmed.

Noah didn't just build the ark—he entered it. He brought his family into the place of protection. That means we cannot merely construct spiritual environments—we must live in them ourselves. Our children are not just listening to our instructions; they are watching our example. If we want them to prioritize God's presence, we must do the same. If we want them to value prayer and the Word, they must see those things in our daily lives. Noah wasn't a perfect man, but he was a righteous one. He walked with God. And because of that, his children were preserved.

We also point our children to the one true door—Jesus Christ. The ark had one door. That wasn't just a design—it was a divine message. In John 10:9 (NKJV), Jesus said, "I am the door. If anyone enters by Me, he will be saved." Our prayers must always lead our children to Christ—not to behavior modification or religion but to a relationship with the Savior.

It's also important to remember that Noah did not save the whole world. He saved his household. That is a profound reminder that our first ministry is our family. The world can burden us, but we are responsible for our homes. The greatest evangelism you will ever do may not be overseas or in front of crowds—it may be in the quiet moments around your dinner table, in bedtime prayers, and in how you respond when life is hard. Your children are learning what faith looks like by how you live it in front of them.

In a world that is building towers of rebellion, we are called to build arks of obedience. The culture around us celebrates independence from God, moral relativism, and the rejection of biblical truth. But as believers, we are called to something different. Like Noah, we are to be set apart, not isolated in fear but consecrated in purpose. We are not hiding from the world—we are preparing our children to shine in it. We are equipping them to carry the presence of God into their schools, friendships, and futures.

Building an ark also means teaching our children to discern the times. Noah's obedience was tied to revelation. He didn't guess that something was coming—he knew because God told him. In the same way, we must be attentive to what the Spirit is saying. We must teach our children to recognize truth, resist deception, and remain rooted when everything around them is shifting. They must learn to walk by the Spirit, to hear God's voice for themselves, and to obey even when it's difficult.

The ark was not only a place of safety—it was a place of waiting. For many days, Noah and his family were inside the ark before the rain even began. And after the rain stopped, they remained inside until God permitted them to leave. This teaches us patience. Building and living in an ark is not glamorous. It is marked by obedience to the unseen. It is a life of faith, not spectacle. Sometimes, our children will question why we live differently. Why don't we watch what others watch? Why do we prioritize church? Why do we say no to certain things? The answer is simple: we are building something sacred. We are not conforming to the pattern of this world—we are preparing them for something eternal.

Romans 12:2 (NKJV) says, "And do not be conformed to this world, but be transformed by the renewing of your mind." Teaching our children to live with renewed minds means we expose them continually to God's truth. Their minds are being shaped daily—by media, school, friends, and experiences. If we do not intentionally engage with their thoughts, the world will disciple them for us. Building an ark includes renewing their minds with Scripture, equipping them to think biblically, and helping them apply truth to real life.

We must also build arks of emotional and spiritual safety. Our homes should be places where our children feel safe asking questions, expressing their doubts, and processing life through a biblical lens. We do not shame them for wrestling with truth—we guide them toward it.

The ark must have windows. There must be light. There must be air. We don't seal them off from the world completely, but we prepare them for it. We build trust. We listen. We point them back to the Word again and again, showing them that God is not intimidated by their questions or struggles.

When the flood finally came, Noah's ark rose above the judgment. It wasn't destroyed—it floated. That is what faith does. It lifts us above the chaos. It preserves us in the middle of a crisis. When we build our lives and our families on the Word, we are not exempt from trouble, but we are kept through it. Jesus said in Matthew 7:24–25 (NKJV), "Therefore whoever hears these sayings of Mine, and does them, I will liken him to a wise man who built his house on the rock: and the rain descended, the floods came, and the winds blew and beat on that house, and it did not fall, for it was founded on the rock." Our obedience becomes the strength of our children's future. Our trust becomes their training ground.

The ark also had one door. Just one. God Himself sealed that door, and it reminds us of something even more important: there is one door to salvation—Jesus. In John 10:9, Jesus said, "I am the door. If anyone enters by Me, he will be saved." As we build spiritual arks, we must continually point our children to Jesus. Not just to morality - not just to religious duty, but to the living Savior who loves them, died for them, was raised from the dead for them, and invites them into a relationship. He is not only their Rescuer—He is their Friend, Shepherd, and King.

As your children grow, their understanding will deepen. But even in the early years, you are laying the foundation. Don't underestimate the power of repetition. The same story read again. The same Scripture is spoken each night. The same prayer whispered over their sleeping heads. These are beams in the ark. These are seeds of faith. Galatians 6:9 (NKJV) encourages us, "And let us not grow weary while doing good, for in due season we shall reap if we do not lose heart." Parenting with intentionality takes endurance. But it will bear fruit.

Eventually, the waters receded, and Noah's family stepped out of the ark into a new world. The ark was not a prison—it was a vessel of transition. Your children will not stay under your roof forever. One day, they will step out into their callings, relationships, and decisions. What you build now will determine how they weather those transitions. If you've built with truth, grace, and prayer, they will carry those beams with them. They may even build arks of their own one day—for their children.

Let us be parents who live with vision. Let us build not just for today but for tomorrow. Let us prepare our children not just for survival but for spiritual victory. The rain may fall, but the righteous will rise. And when we build by faith, according to God's Word, we will see His promises fulfilled—not only in us but in every life sheltered by the ark we have built.

Chapter 7
Praying the Word over Your Children

There is no more powerful way to pray for your children than by using the Word of God. Scripture is not only God's revealed will—it is God's living voice. When we pray Scripture, we are not simply expressing our hopes but declaring eternal truth that carries divine authority. We are not pleading for uncertain outcomes but standing on promises already spoken and sealed in heaven. God's Word does not expire, weaken, or return void. It is timeless, effective, and supernatural. That is why parents who learn to pray the Word over their children step into a realm of prayer rooted in faith, not fear, and anchored in God's power rather than their own.

The idea of praying Scripture may seem intimidating to some, especially those who are not sure where to begin. But it is not complicated. It starts with finding promises in God's Word that speak to your child's life—promises about protection, wisdom, salvation, purpose, peace, and identity. These verses become the foundation of your prayers. Instead of simply saying, "God, please protect my child," you can say, "Lord, I thank You that Your angels are given charge over my child to keep them in all their ways" (Psalm 91:11). Instead of praying, "Help my child not to be afraid," you can declare, "God has not given my child a spirit of fear, but of power and love and a sound mind" 2 Timothy 1:7 (NKJV). The Word becomes your script, your shield, and your sword.

When we pray the Word, we are praying God's language. Isaiah 55:11 (NKJV) tells us, "So shall My word be that goes forth from My mouth; it shall not return to Me void, but it shall accomplish what I please." This means that when we speak God's Word in prayer, we are releasing something that has the power to create change. Our words, on their own, are limited. But God's Word is creative. It is active. It is full of life. It does not need our eloquence—it only needs our agreement.

Children are living in a time of great spiritual pressure. The world is not passive toward them—it is actively shaping their beliefs, desires, and identity. That is why it is more important than ever for parents to be intentional in prayer. The enemy comes to steal, kill, and destroy, but Jesus came that our children might have life and have it more abundantly (John 10:10). When we pray the Word, we are not reacting in fear—we are taking spiritual authority. We are speaking life into the places where the enemy would love to sow confusion, fear, or despair. We are not helpless spectators. We are intercessors standing in the gap.

Prayer that is built on God's Word is not just powerful—it is precise. It targets specific areas of a child's life from heaven's perspective. If your child is struggling with insecurity, you can pray Psalm 139:14 over them: "I will praise You, for I am fearfully and wonderfully made." If they are facing pressure from peers or wrestling with identity, they can pray Ephesians 2:10: "For we are His workmanship, created in Christ Jesus for good works, which God prepared beforehand." If they are anxious, you can pray Philippians 4:7 (NKJV): "And the peace of God, which surpasses all understanding, will guard your hearts and minds through Christ Jesus."

You are not simply asking for change—you are declaring it. And when you do so in faith, heaven responds. Hebrews 4:12 reminds us that the Word of God is "living and powerful, and sharper than any two-edged sword." This means that every time you pray Scripture, you are swinging a sword in the spiritual realm. You are cutting through lies. You are breaking chains. You are building a wall of protection around your child's heart and mind. You may not see the results immediately, but the battle is being fought and won in the spirit.

There is also a renewing effect on the parent who prays the Word. As you speak God's truth, your own heart is strengthened. Your perspective shifts from worry to worship, from anxiety to assurance. Faith rises as you remind yourself of what God has said. Romans 10:17 (NKJV) says, "Faith comes by hearing, and hearing by the word of God." When you hear yourself praying the Word, your spirit is fed. Your doubts are silenced. Your authority is restored. And your prayers take on a new level of confidence.

Praying the Word is not a formula—it is a relationship. It is communion with the God who made your child, who knows their future, and who has promised to guide and guard them. When you speak His Word back to Him, you are not informing Him of anything—He already knows. But you are inviting His promises into your present. You are opening the door for His kingdom to come and His will to be done in your child's life.

You can begin this practice in simple ways. Choose a handful of Scriptures that speak directly to the areas your child is facing. Write them down. Speak them aloud in prayer. Place them where you can see them throughout the day. Use them during bedtime prayers or while driving to school. Repeat them with your child. Let them hear the sound of God's Word coming from your lips. Let it become familiar, comforting, and powerful. Over time, those words will become part of their vocabulary. They will learn to speak the Word for themselves. And that is when prayer becomes a legacy.

There may be times when your child doesn't seem to respond to your efforts. They may roll their eyes, show resistance, or seem indifferent. Do not be discouraged. The Word is still working. Isaiah 55:10–11 compares God's Word to rain and snow that water the earth: "It shall not return to Me void… it shall prosper in the thing for which I sent it." You may not see the fruit yet, but the seed is in the ground. God is faithful to bring the harvest. Your prayers are never wasted.

You don't need to be a Bible scholar to pray the Word of God. You don't need perfect phrasing. You don't need long, complicated sentences. What you need is a willing heart and the courage to speak. God honors your sincerity. He hears every whisper, every declaration, every verse spoken in love and faith. He is not grading your performance—He is responding to your heart. And when your heart is aligned with His Word, there is power released.

This kind of praying builds spiritual confidence in your child. They may not always understand the words at first, but they will recognize the tone of truth. They will begin to associate prayer with hope, Scripture with strength, and your voice with love. Over time, this creates a spiritual atmosphere in your home that is difficult to shake. It becomes a sanctuary in a chaotic world. A refuge filled with light and truth.

As your child grows, continue to pray the Word over their changing seasons. As they begin school, pray for wisdom, favor, and discernment. As they navigate friendships, pray for godly influences and a strong identity. As they approach adolescence, pray for purity, courage, and a sense of purpose. As they step into adulthood, pray for destiny, protection, and intimacy with God. There is a Scripture for every stage. A promise for every need. And as you pray through the seasons, you will see God's hand at work in ways you never imagined.

The beauty of praying the Word is that it doesn't stop with one generation. As your children hear and learn, they will begin to pray Scripture over their own lives and eventually over their own families. The declarations you make today will echo into the future. Psalm 102:18 says, "This will be written for the generation to come, that a people yet to be created may praise the Lord." Your prayers, rooted in the Word, are building a spiritual inheritance that cannot be taken away.

Even in the face of crisis, the Word provides an anchor. When your child is hurting, lost, or far from God, the promises you've prayed are still active. They are like homing beacons, calling them back to truth. The prodigal son, though far away, never stopped being his father's child. And when he returned, he came home to a father who had never stopped believing. Luke 15:20 says, "But when he was still a great way off, his father saw him and had compassion." This is the heart of God, and it is the heart we carry when we pray His Word over our children.

If you've never prayed Scripture before, now is the time to begin. You don't need to know every verse. Just start with one. Open your Bible, find a promise, and speak it aloud. Say it with faith. Say it with love. Say it as a parent who believes in the power of God's Word. Let that Word shape your prayers, guide your thoughts, and fill your home. And over time, you will see the fruit.

The Word of God is not chained by circumstances, limited by age, or weakened by delay. It is alive. It is working. And when you pray it over your children, you are aligning yourself with the very heart of heaven. You are partnering with the purposes of God. And you are building a legacy of faith that will outlive you and bless every generation to come.

Chapter 8

The Blessing of the Righteous Upon Their Children

There is a divine pattern woven throughout Scripture that cannot be ignored: God blesses the children of the righteous. This truth is not merely a poetic ideal or a hopeful sentiment; it is a spiritual law rooted in the very character of God. From Genesis to Revelation, we see that those who walk uprightly before the Lord carry with them a generational blessing that reaches far beyond their own lives. When a man or woman chooses to live a life of righteousness, they are not just securing favor for themselves but also opening the floodgates of blessing over their children, their grandchildren, and even future generations they may never see.

Psalm 112 paints a powerful picture of this principle: "Blessed is the man who fears the Lord, who delights greatly in His commandments. His descendants will be mighty on earth; the generation of the upright will be blessed" (Psalm 112:1–2, NKJV). The Word does not say his descendants *might* be mighty; it says they *will* be. This is not a suggestion; it is a promise. When righteousness marks a parent's life, blessings mark the lives of their children. It may not always look immediate. It may not always follow a straight line. But the Word of the Lord will stand.

Righteousness, in this context, is not about being flawless; rather, it is about being faithful. It is not about outward perfection or religious appearance. It is about walking in a relationship with God, loving what He loves, and living according to His truth. It is about humility, repentance, faithfulness, and obedience. It is about choosing God's ways over the world's, even when it comes at a cost. And when a parent lives this way, heaven responds.

Proverbs 20:7 echoes this idea: "The righteous man walks in his integrity; his children are blessed after him." Notice the word *after*. This suggests that the blessing may follow the parent's life and extend directly into the lives of their children. It may manifest in protection, in provision, in favor, in wisdom, or in open doors that would otherwise remain closed. It may manifest as a sensitivity to God's voice, an early calling, or a supernatural protection from harm. These are not coincidences. They are the fruit of living in alignment with God's heart.

Even the structure of God's covenants reveals His generational nature. When God made a covenant with Abraham, He said, "I will bless you... and in you all the families of the earth shall be blessed" (Genesis 12:2–3 NKJV). This wasn't just about Abraham's immediate life but a whole legacy. His walk of faith would ripple across history and reach nations. Righteousness always leaves a trail of blessings in its wake.

There is a beautiful picture of this in the life of David. Despite his failures, David remained a man after God's heart. His life was marked by worship, repentance, and trust. Because of this, God made an eternal covenant with him. What is striking is that long after David was gone, God continued to bless his descendants, not because they were always righteous, but because *he* had been. In 1 Kings 11:34, God says of Solomon, "However, I will not take the whole kingdom out of his hand, because I have made him ruler all the days of his life for the sake of My servant David." The blessing on David's life outlived him. His legacy of righteousness created a covering for his children, even in their rebellion.

This is the mystery and mercy of God: that He honors the lives of the righteous in such a way that their children reap the benefits. This truth should encourage every parent who is living faithfully, even when they feel unnoticed or unappreciated. Your prayers, your obedience, your sacrificial love... they matter; they shape your life and plant seeds in the lives of your children that will grow into blessings in their time.

It is important to understand that this blessing is not transactional but relational. We do not live righteously to manipulate God into blessing our children. We live righteously because we love God, and in doing so, we align ourselves with the flow of His blessing. Our lives become rivers through which His goodness flows to the next generation. We become carriers of legacy.

Psalm 37:25–26 reinforces this idea: "I have been young, and now am old, yet I have not seen the righteous forsaken, nor his descendants begging bread. He is ever merciful and lends, and his descendants are blessed." This is generational testimony. The blessing of the righteous includes provision, mercy, and abundance for themselves and for those who follow. The children of the righteous carry a unique spiritual inheritance. Even if they stray for a time, the prayers and faith of their parents follow them like a shadow.

One of the most precious truths in Scripture is that the blessing of the righteous is not limited to biological children. It extends to spiritual children, to those we mentor, disciple, and pour into. Paul referred to Timothy as his "true son in the faith" (1 Timothy 1:2 NKJV). His influence on Timothy's life was profound, and it bore fruit in the kingdom of God. If you are someone who has no children of your own, know this: your righteousness can still leave a generational impact. Every life you touch becomes part of your spiritual legacy.

The blessing also works through spoken words. Throughout Scripture, righteous parents pronounced blessings over their children. Isaac blessed Jacob. Jacob blessed his twelve sons. Even in the New Testament, Jesus laid hands on children and blessed them. Our words have power. When we bless our children intentionally, we are not simply offering kind wishes; we are speaking life, truth, and destiny into their lives. We are declaring what God has already written and aligning ourselves with His purposes. This is not superstition; it is spiritual authority.

Job, a man described as blameless and upright, understood this. He interceded for his children continually. Job 1:5 says, "Job would send and sanctify them... and he would rise early in the morning and offer burnt offerings according to the number of them all." He feared God not only for himself but for his family. His righteousness covered his children. He took their spiritual well-being seriously, and heaven recorded his actions.

Parents may wonder how to walk in this blessing and pass it on practically. The answer is found in daily faithfulness. Seek God. Love His Word. Repent quickly. Forgive freely. Worship genuinely. Speak truth. Live humbly. Be quick to listen and slow to speak. Create a home where Jesus is not just mentioned but honored, where grace is not just talked about but practiced, and where prayer is not an obligation but a refuge. These simple, steady practices build a life of righteousness and attract the blessings of God.

There may be seasons where the blessing seems hidden, where children struggle. Where it feels like the promises are delayed, but don't be deceived by appearances. God is not finished. The story is still being written. The same God who watched over David's descendants, who honored Job's intercessions, and who fulfilled His Word to Abraham is watching over your family too. Galatians 6:9 encourages us, "And let us not grow weary while doing good, for in due season we shall reap if we do not lose heart." The harvest is coming.

Even when children rebel or walk away, the seed remains. The blessing of the righteous is not easily uprooted. It is not fragile. It is not forgotten. It is held in the hands of a covenant-keeping God. He sees every tear, every late-night prayer, every act of love given in secret. And He is faithful to honor it all. Isaiah 59:21 offers this incredible promise: "As for Me," says the Lord, "this is My covenant with them: My Spirit who is upon you, and My words which I have put in your mouth shall not depart from your mouth, nor from the mouth of your descendants." This is the legacy of righteousness. It is a river that never runs dry.

Let every righteous parent be encouraged. Your life matters more than you know. Your walk with God is shaping the course of history. Your faith is building something eternal. And your children, no matter where they are today, are covered by a blessing that cannot be broken, erased, or outlived. Keep walking. Keep praying. Keep believing. For the blessing of the righteous shall rest upon their children, and the God who promised is faithful to bring it to pass.

Chapter 9

God's Will to Save Your Children

The desire to see our children saved is one of the deepest cries in a parent's heart. It's not merely a hope or a wish; it is a longing so profound that it touches every prayer, every decision, and every moment we spend with them. But more powerful than our desire is God's own will. The good news is that our longing for our children's salvation aligns perfectly with God's will. We do not have to beg God to care for us. We do not need to convince Him to intervene. The truth is that He wants our children saved even more than we do. Salvation is His idea, His mission, and His promise. Knowing this transforms how we pray, how we wait, and how we believe.

God is eager to give. Scripture makes this abundantly clear. In 2 Peter 3:9, we read, "The Lord is not slack concerning His promise, as some count slackness, but is long-suffering toward us, not willing that any should perish but that all should come to repentance." That word *all* includes your children. God does not exclude your son because of rebellion or your daughter because of doubt. He is not indifferent to their resistance or blind to their potential. He is patient, persistent, and deeply invested. He is a Father who never stops pursuing.

The enemy would love for parents to believe that some children are too far gone or too hard-hearted to ever return to God. But such thoughts do not come from heaven. They come from fear, which is the opposite of faith. The truth is God sees the end from the beginning. He knows every detour and delay, and yet He still calls them His own. He still extends His hand. He still stands at the door and knocks. Salvation is not limited by age, behavior, or time. As long as there is breath, there is hope. Isaiah 49:25 declares, "For I will contend with him who contends with you, and I will save your children." This is not a generic blessing but a personal promise.

Parents who understand that salvation is God's will can pray with boldness and certainty. We are not trying to persuade God to act against His nature; we are joining with His heart. We are aligning our intercession with His eternal purpose. First Timothy 2:3–4 says, "For this is good and acceptable in the sight of God our Savior, who desires all men to be saved and to come to the knowledge of the truth." This desire includes our sons and daughters. When we pray for their salvation, we are praying for the very heartbeat of heaven.

Parents need to speak life, not death, over their children. Words matter. If we constantly confess doubt and despair, we are cooperating with the enemy's plan. But when we speak God's Word over our children, we partner with the Spirit of God. Proverbs 18:21 tells us, "Death and life are in the power of the tongue." Our words can build a path for our children to walk on, even when they seem far from it. We may not be able to control their choices, but we can shape the atmosphere around them with faith-filled declarations of God's promises.

The story of the prodigal son in Luke 15 reveals the heart of the Father more than it reveals the son's rebellion. The father does not chase the son down the road in fear; he watches and waits with expectation. He keeps the home prepared. He remains confident in love. And when the son finally returns, the father runs to meet him. That is how God feels about our children. He is not condemning them from a distance; He is looking for them with compassion. He is ready to restore. His heart never changes.

Salvation is more than forgiveness; it is transformation. It is the complete work of redemption, renewal, and relationship with God. That work begins in the spirit, but it touches every part of life. When we pray for our children's salvation, we are asking God not only to save them from sin but also to call them to a purpose. We are praying for identity to be restored, for destiny to be awakened, and for lives to be marked by the presence of Jesus. This is not small; it is kingdom-sized.

We also must recognize that the seeds of salvation are often planted long before we see the fruit. A child who seems uninterested in spiritual things may still be carrying the seeds of truth deep in their heart. Seeds of Scripture, of past prayers, of conversations and quiet moments. Galatians 6:9 (NKJV) encourages us, "Let us not grow weary while doing good, for in due season we shall reap if we do not lose heart." The key is not to give up. The harvest is coming.

There is also great power in a parent's spiritual authority. When you stand in prayer for your child, you are not a bystander. You are a gatekeeper. You have the authority to speak life, to cancel the enemy's plans, to declare God's promises, and to create a spiritual covering over their lives. Even when they don't recognize it, even when they resist it, your prayers matter. Your voice in the spirit is heard in heaven. Your declarations of faith shake the darkness.

One of the most powerful examples of this is found in the Book of Job. Job was described as a righteous man, and one of his daily practices was to offer sacrifices and intercede on behalf of his children. Job 1:5 says, "Thus Job did regularly." He did not wait until his children were in crisis. He covered them in prayer every day. He understood that the spiritual condition of his children was worth fighting for, even if it was behind the scenes. That is the call of every parent to be a consistent voice in heaven on behalf of their children.

Salvation is also generational. God often works through family lines. When Paul and Silas were in prison, they told the jailer, "Believe on the Lord Jesus Christ, and you will be saved, you and your household" (Acts 16:31 NKJV). This was not a coincidence; it was a pattern. God delights in bringing salvation to whole families. He honors legacy. He responds to faith that spans generations. And He delights in seeing His promises fulfilled across family lines.

For those who feel like they have failed, take heart. Your mistakes do not limit God. His grace is greater than your past. You may feel that you missed opportunities, said the wrong things, or drifted at a crucial time. But God is a Redeemer. He restores the years that the enemy has stolen (Joel 2:25). He can do in one moment what we could not do in years of trying. His Spirit is not bound by time. It is never too late.

As you continue to pray, remind yourself of who God is. He is faithful. He is merciful. He is a Savior. He is a Father who seeks the lost and rejoices over every return. Luke 19:10 says, "For the Son of Man has come to seek and to save that which was lost" (NKJV). He is still seeking. He is still saving. And He will not stop pursuing your child.

Make space in your home and your heart for God to move. Worship openly. Share testimonies. Speak Scripture. Live your faith authentically. Create an environment where grace is real and the door is always open. Let your life preach the gospel without words. Let your love be unconditional. Let your hope remain unshaken.

In time, your children will remember. They will recall the prayers, the love, the truth. And even if they take the long road home, they will not outrun the Spirit of God. He is the One who convicts, who comforts, who calls. And He is working, even now.

God's will is clear and distinct. He desires that your children know Him, love Him, and walk in His ways. He is able to save, to deliver, to restore. And He is faithful to complete what He begins.

You can rest in His promises. You can stand in the gap. You can trust His timing. And you can declare with confidence that your children will be saved because He promised it. And He is faithful.

Chapter 10
Promises of Spiritual Outpouring for Your Descendants

God's promises to His people have always extended beyond the immediate moment. He is a generational God, a covenant-keeping Father whose plans extend not just to individuals but to entire family lines. As believing parents, we are not only called to raise our children with wisdom and love; we are invited to believe for something greater: a spiritual outpouring on our descendants. This promise is not based on our ability or perfection but on the enduring Word of God. It is God's declared intention to move powerfully in the lives of our children and their children, to pour out His Spirit, His presence, and His power on all who come after us. And this is not a distant hope. It is a promise to be embraced now.

In Acts 2, after the Holy Spirit was poured out on the day of Pentecost, Peter stood up and declared, "For the promise is to you and your children, and to all who are afar off, as many as the Lord our God will call" (Acts 2:39). He was quoting the prophet Joel and applying the Word to a new moment. This declaration wasn't just a passing encouragement; it was a divine announcement. The outpouring of the Spirit was not a one-time event for the apostles. It was the beginning of something that would continue for generations. The Spirit was poured out not only for the believers gathered in that moment but also for their children, for those who hadn't even been born yet.

Joel had prophesied it centuries earlier: "And it shall come to pass afterward that I will pour out My Spirit on all flesh; your sons and your daughters shall prophesy... And also on My menservants and My maidservants, I will pour out My Spirit in those days" (Joel 2:28–29). Notice the language... your sons, your daughters. This is personal. It's not just a corporate move; it's a family promise. God is not only concerned with revival in churches or communities; He desires revival in homes, in households, and in the hearts of children raised to know and walk with Him.

This promise of outpouring is for every believer who dares to believe that God will move powerfully in their family. It is not reserved for those who have perfect histories or flawless parenting records. It is for those who hold on to the Word of God and pray with expectation. It is for those who stand in faith and say, "Lord, if You promised to pour out Your Spirit on our sons and daughters, I will believe until I see it." This kind of faith is not passive. It is active. It prays, it declares, it waits, and it prepares.

Many parents feel overwhelmed by the culture surrounding their children. The noise, the distraction, the darkness. But God is not intimidated by culture. He is not hindered by rebellion or slowed by confusion. In fact, He often does His greatest work in the darkest hours. The same God who poured out His Spirit on the early church during a time of political unrest and religious opposition continues to pour out His Spirit today. And He has not forgotten your children.

Isaiah 44:3 contains a beautiful promise: "For I will pour water on him who is thirsty, and floods on the dry ground; I will pour My Spirit on your descendants, and My blessing on your offspring." What a declaration. This is God speaking through the prophet, promising to meet dry places with floods, to satisfy thirst, and to pour out His Spirit, not just on the individual but also on their descendants. This is a picture of revival that begins in one life and flows like a river into future generations.

As parents, our role is not only to raise our children morally but to position them spiritually. We are called to prepare the soil of their hearts to receive the rain of the Spirit. That means exposing them to the presence of God, teaching them the Word, modeling prayer, cultivating a hunger for God, and praying with expectation. It also means we believe, even when we don't see immediate results, that God is faithful to His promise. The same Spirit who hovered over the waters in Genesis now hovers over the hearts of our children, waiting for the Word of the Lord to be spoken.

The outpouring of the Holy Spirit is not just about emotional experiences or temporary moments of excitement. It is about transformation. When the Spirit is poured out, hearts are softened, lives are changed, and boldness replaces fear. Our children were created not just to survive the times they live in but to be filled with the power of God and to carry His presence wherever they go. The promise of spiritual outpouring is not merely protection from evil; it is empowerment for purpose.

God's heart is for families to be filled with the Spirit together. In Acts 10, when Peter preached to Cornelius's household, the Holy Spirit fell on all who heard the Word. Not just Cornelius. Not just a few. The entire household experienced the outpouring. This is what God wants to do again and again: fill homes with His glory, pour out His Spirit on young and old, and ignite families with a fire that cannot be quenched. When the Spirit is poured out, barriers fall. Generations unite. Faith is transferred. Destiny is awakened.

Some parents feel that their families are too fractured to make such a promise. But God's promises are not limited by our past or present condition. He is a God who restores, who redeems, and who brings beauty out of brokenness. If your child is far from God, the promise still stands. If your family has faced turmoil or division, the promise still stands. If you have made mistakes, the promise remains in effect. Isaiah 59:21 declares, "As for Me," says the Lord, "this is My covenant with them: My Spirit who is upon you, and My words which I have put in your mouth shall not depart from your mouth, nor from the mouth of your descendants… from this time and forevermore." This is an eternal promise.

We must teach our children that the Holy Spirit is not a distant concept but a present Helper. He is the One who convicts, comforts, empowers, and leads. He is not reserved for pastors or missionaries. He is for every believer, including the youngest. Children are not too young to experience the Spirit. In fact, they often receive with greater simplicity and trust. Jesus Himself said, "Let the little children come to Me and do not forbid them; for of such is the kingdom of heaven" (Matthew 19:14). The outpouring begins when we stop underestimating what God can do in a child.

This promise of outpouring also invites us to contend for more. We don't just want our children to know about God; we want them to encounter Him. We want them to hear His voice, walk in His wisdom, dream dreams, and see visions. We want them to be filled with the Spirit, led by the Spirit, and empowered to stand strong in a world that is shaky. We are not content with religious routine; we want revival in our homes.

To prepare for a spiritual outpouring, we must first steward our own lives. Are we thirsty for the Spirit ourselves? Are we creating space for God to move? Are we modeling hunger, repentance, obedience, and faith? The river of outpouring often flows through those who are willing to be vessels. Our children need to see that walking in the Spirit is powerful. When they see the fruit of the Spirit in our lives - love, joy, peace, patience, kindness, goodness, faithfulness, gentleness, and self-control - they begin to desire it for themselves.

Pray specifically for your children to receive the Holy Spirit. Pray that their hearts would be tender, that their ears would be open, and that their spirits would be responsive. Ask God to remove distractions, to silence the lies of the enemy, and to cultivate holy desire. Speak the promises aloud. Declare Joel 2:28 over your home. Write down Acts 2:39 and put it where you can see it every day. Make room for the Spirit in your daily life. Worship openly. Welcome His presence.

There may be resistance at first. There may be seasons where things feel quiet. But keep believing. Keep declaring. Keep preparing. The rain will come. The promise is sure. God has not changed His mind. He is still the One who pours out His Spirit. And He delights in doing it through families, through generations, through simple, faithful people who say yes.

You are not just raising a child; you are raising a career of revival. You are preparing a vessel for the Spirit of God. And the promise of outpouring is not just for someone else's family. It is for you.

Chapter 11

Prophetic Encouragement and Intercessory Prayer

When it comes to standing in faith for our children, God has equipped us with two powerful spiritual tools: prophetic encouragement and intercessory prayer. These are not reserved for pastors, prophets, or spiritual leaders. They are available to every believing parent, grandparent, or guardian who desires to see God's purposes fulfilled in their children's lives. These two expressions of spiritual authority work together: one speaks life and vision into the future, and the other labors in the Spirit to bring that future into reality.

Prophetic encouragement is not about predicting the future; it is about offering guidance and support. It is about declaring what God has already revealed in His Word and by His Spirit. It is the ability to see beyond and through current circumstances and speak the truth about who your child is in God's eyes. When we prophetically encourage our children, we are not flattering them or feeding their egos but aligning our words with heaven's view of them. We affirm their identity, calling, and value in a world that constantly tries to redefine them.

The Apostle Paul taught the early church that prophecy was meant to edify, exhort, and comfort (1 Corinthians 14:3). That is the spirit of prophetic encouragement in the home. We speak words that build up, inspire, and reassure. When a child is struggling with fear, we remind them of God's faithfulness. When they're uncertain about their purpose, we remind them of Jeremiah 29:11: "For I know the thoughts that I think toward you… thoughts of peace and not of evil, to give you a future and a hope." When they feel like they don't belong, we declare Ephesians 2:10: "For we are His workmanship, created in Christ Jesus for good works."

These words aren't just affirmations; they are declarations. They are prophetic because they speak beyond what is visible and reach into

56

what is possible. We call out the gold that God has placed within our children, even when all we see on the surface are struggles or shortcomings. We don't deny reality, but we proclaim the truth of God that is greater than the temporary challenges.

Prophetic encouragement is rooted in the promises of Scripture. We do not invent words; we agree with God's words. We declare them with authority and love, not out of desperation but out of conviction. Our children may not always seem to listen or respond, but the Word is doing its work. Isaiah 55:11 reminds us that God's Word "shall not return to Me void, but it shall accomplish what I please, and it shall prosper in the thing for which I sent it." Every time you speak Scripture over your children, you are sending out a divine assignment. You are shaping their spiritual atmosphere and their future.

Intercessory prayer is the other side of this coin. If prophetic encouragement declares what God has said, intercessory prayer contends for its fulfillment. To intercede is to stand in the gap, to take up a position between heaven and earth on behalf of another. It is one of the most selfless and powerful expressions of love a parent can offer. When we intercede for our children, we are not only praying from emotion but from spiritual authority. We are stepping into the place of a watchman, a warrior, a priest.

Scripture is filled with examples of intercessors. Abraham interceded for Lot. Moses stood in the gap for the Israelites. Hannah poured out her soul for a child she had not yet conceived. Job prayed daily for his sons and daughters. Jesus Himself intercedes for us even now, seated at the right hand of the Father (Romans 8:34). Intercession is not just a spiritual exercise; it is a sacred calling. And when we pray for our children with perseverance, faith, and specificity, we are joining Jesus in His ministry of love and advocacy.

Intercessory prayer is often birthed in pain. It comes from seeing our children go through hardship, confusion, temptation, or rebellion. It comes from watching them struggle with things we cannot fix. But instead of giving in to despair, we bring their names before the throne of God. We cry out for mercy, for intervention, for protection. And God hears. Psalm 34:17 says, "The righteous cry out, and the Lord hears and delivers them out of all their troubles." The prayers of a righteous parent are powerful. They reach beyond what our hands can touch. They travel into the heart of God and release His hand into the lives of our children.

There is also a prophetic dimension to intercession. Often, as we pray, God reveals things about our children that we would not have known otherwise. He may give us insight into their struggles, direction for their future, or warnings about dangers they cannot yet see. This is not for control but for covering. We don't use prophetic intercession to manipulate; we use it to protect, to guide, and to love with discernment. The Holy Spirit is our helper in this. Romans 8:26 assures us that "the Spirit Himself makes intercession for us with groanings which cannot be uttered." When we don't know how to pray, He does.

Some seasons of intercession are marked by joy, while tears mark others. There are times when we sense victory quickly and times when we must persevere for years. But no prayer offered in faith is ever lost. Revelation 5:8 gives us a picture of golden bowls in heaven "full of incense, which are the prayers of the saints." Our prayers are being collected, remembered, and answered in God's perfect time. The intercessions of a parent are never wasted.

Combining prophetic encouragement with intercessory prayer creates a powerful dynamic in your home. Your children begin to feel not just loved but seen. They understand that they are not alone in their journey. They sense that a spiritual safety net surrounds them, pulling them upward even when they fall. This doesn't mean they will never struggle, but it means they will never be without a spiritual lifeline.

Prophetic encouragement can happen in quiet moments. A hand on the shoulder, a gentle word in the car, a Scripture note left on the mirror. Intercession often happens when no one sees: early in the morning, late at night, during daily routines. But heaven sees. God responds. And over time, these spiritual investments yield fruit that lasts.

Our children are not just navigating a natural world; they are living in a spiritual one. They face temptations, battles, questions, and wounds. They need encouragement that speaks to their spirit and prayer that battles on their behalf. We must speak life into them and pray for life around them. We must prophesy their identity and intercede for their protection. We must remind them of who they are and fight for who they are becoming.

When our children see us operate in prophetic encouragement and intercession, they learn to do the same. They learn to listen for God's voice and speak His Word with boldness. They learn to carry others in prayer. They learn to stand on God's promises and fight spiritual battles with spiritual weapons. They learn that faith is not a Sunday concept; it is a daily lifestyle.

Let us be the parents who do not merely observe our children's lives from the sidelines. Let us be those who step into the arena with them, cheering them on, lifting them, covering them in prayer, and declaring over them the destiny that God has written. Let our homes be filled with the sound of blessing, the strength of prayer, and the peace of God's presence, for, in doing so, we are raising not just good children; we are raising sons and daughters filled with the Spirit, rooted in truth, and equipped for every good work.

Chapter 12
Spiritual Protection for Your Children

In a world filled with danger, distraction, and deception, one of the greatest concerns for any parent is the safety of their children. Yet beyond the visible threats lies an even more urgent and often overlooked need: spiritual protection. Every day, our children face not just physical challenges but spiritual ones. They are bombarded with messages, influenced by voices, and exposed to pressures that shape their beliefs, behavior, and identity. But as believing parents, we are not helpless. God has given us powerful promises of spiritual protection, and we are called to actively engage in that protection through prayer, truth, and obedience.

The world is not a neutral place. Scripture is clear that we are in the midst of a spiritual battle. Ephesians 6:12 tells us, "For we do not wrestle against flesh and blood, but against principalities, against powers, against the rulers of the darkness of this age." This is not a call to fear but rather a call to awareness. It is a reminder that behind every temptation, every confusion, every sudden shift in behavior or thought. There may be a deeper spiritual influence at work. But the good news is that we are not without weapons. God has given us everything we need to stand firm and cover our children in divine protection.

One of the clearest pictures of God's protective promise is found in Psalm 91. It is a passage every parent should become familiar with and speak often over their children. "He who dwells in the secret place of the Most High shall abide under the shadow of the Almighty… He shall cover you with His feathers, and under His wings, you shall take refuge… For He shall give His angels charge over you, to keep you in all your ways" (Psalm 91:1, 4, 11). These are not poetic words alone; they are declarations of divine defense. When we pray Psalm 91 over our children, we are invoking the covenantal care of God. We are asking

Him to shield them not only from harm but from spiritual forces that seek to derail their purpose.

Angelic protection is one of God's great gifts to His people. Hebrews 1:14 says that angels are "ministering spirits sent forth to minister for those who will inherit salvation." That includes our children. Even when we cannot be physically present, God can assign angels to guard their steps, to warn them, and to intervene in ways we may never see. Many parents have testimonies of divine protection in moments when danger was near. But whether we see it or not, we can trust that God is faithful to His Word.

Spiritual protection also comes through the armor of God. Ephesians 6:13–17 outlines this armor: the belt of truth, the breastplate of righteousness, the shoes of the gospel of peace, the shield of faith, the helmet of salvation, and the sword of the Spirit. As parents, we can teach our children how to "put on" this armor daily, not through ritual but through relationship. We help them grow in truth by teaching them the Word of God. We protect their hearts with righteousness by modeling integrity. We guide their feet in peace by living in forgiveness. We shield their minds with faith by declaring God's promises. And we equip their hands with the Word by helping them memorize and meditate on Scripture.

The home is the first line of defense for spiritual protection. What we allow into our homes through media, conversation, and atmosphere either fortifies or weakens our children's spiritual defenses. We must be discerning about the environment we create. Is our home a place where God's presence is welcome? Is prayer normal? Is worship frequent? Is Scripture valued? These things are not just for Sunday; they are the foundation of daily life. When our homes are saturated in God's presence, they become strongholds of peace.

We also must pray specifically. General prayers are beneficial, but specific prayers are even more powerful. Ask God to protect your child's mind from lies and confusion. Pray for protection over their friendships, school, emotions, and choices. Ask the Holy Spirit to expose every hidden attack of the enemy and to give your child spiritual discernment. Speak the blood of Jesus over their lives daily. Revelation 12:11 says, "And they overcame him by the blood of the Lamb and by the word of their testimony." The blood of Jesus is not only for forgiveness but for victory.

Intercessory prayer is one of the greatest acts of spiritual warfare a parent can offer. You may not be able to follow your child into every classroom, every conversation, or every challenge, but your prayers go with them. You can bind what needs to be bound and lose what needs to be loosed. You can call down divine intervention. You can speak confusion into the camp of the enemy and clarity into the heart of your child. You can stand between your child and spiritual danger, even when they are unaware.

Proverbs 18:10 reminds us, "The name of the Lord is a strong tower; the righteous run to it and are safe." When you speak the name of Jesus over your child, you are invoking that tower. You are placing them under a covering that no force of hell can penetrate. There is no safer place than under the authority and protection of the name of Jesus. Use His name often in prayer, in blessing, in declaration.

It's also essential to teach your children how to protect themselves spiritually. Equip them to pray, to resist temptation, to recognize truth from lies, and to stand on the Word of God. Teach them that they are not helpless; they have spiritual authority as children of God. Luke 10:19 says, "Behold, I give you the authority... over all the power of the enemy, and nothing shall by any means hurt you." Even the youngest believers can walk in spiritual power when they understand their identity in Christ.

As your children grow, their spiritual battles will change, but God's protection remains constant. From playground dynamics to teenage temptations to adult decisions, they will need the covering of your prayers and the foundation of your faith. Be their watchman. Be their priest. Be their warrior in the spirit. And never underestimate the influence you have, not just in shaping their character, but in shielding their destiny.

There may be times when your child faces hardship or danger despite your prayers. In those moments, do not lose heart. God's protection does not always look like avoidance; it often looks like preservation through the trial. Daniel was thrown into the lions' den, but he was not harmed. The three Hebrew boys were cast into the fire, but they were not burned. Paul faced shipwreck, beatings, and imprisonment, but he was preserved to fulfill his mission. Sometimes, God delivers us from the fire; other times, He walks with us through it. Either way, His protection is real.

Psalm 121 is another powerful chapter to declare over your children: "The Lord shall preserve you from all evil; He shall preserve your soul. The Lord shall preserve your going out and your coming in from this time forth, and even forevermore" (verses 7–8). That promise covers every season, every journey, every stage of life. It is not just poetic; it is prophetic. Speak it aloud. Let your children hear it. Let them grow up knowing that they are not alone, that they are divinely covered.

Finally, rest in the assurance that God loves your children even more than you do. He sees what you cannot see. He knows what you cannot know. And He is faithful to guard what you entrust to Him. Second Timothy 1:12 declares, "For I know whom I have believed and am persuaded that He is able to keep what I have committed to Him until that Day." Commit your children to Him daily. Trust Him with their lives, their futures, their struggles, and their stories.

Spiritual protection is more about faith and the least about fear. It is not about control instead of covering. And it is about persistence, not perfection. When you pray in faith, declare in confidence, and stand in the promises of God, your children are protected and positioned for victory.

Chapter 13
Praying for Wisdom and Destiny for Our Children

There is no greater privilege or responsibility than to pray for the lives and futures of our children. As believing parents, we are invited to partner with God in the shaping of our children's stories through prayer. We do not do this from a place of fear or anxiety but from a place of confident faith, knowing that the God who formed them in the womb has also written their destiny. Our role is not to control the outcome but to align our hearts with heaven and pray for the three most critical areas of their spiritual journey: their salvation, their wisdom, and their destiny.

Salvation is the starting point of all true life. It is not just about going to heaven one day; it is about being brought into a relationship with the living God here and now. Salvation is the doorway to every promise, every purpose, and every blessing that God has prepared for us. When we pray for our children's salvation, we are not asking for something uncertain; we are laying hold of what is already God's will. Scripture says, "Who desires all men to be saved and to come to the knowledge of the truth" (1 Timothy 2:4). God's desire includes our children. We are not pleading for something outside of His will—we are praying in alignment with His deepest longing.

But salvation is not something we can force. It is a work of the Holy Spirit, born of conviction, revelation, and surrender. That's why our prayers are so vital. We ask God to soften our children's hearts, to open their spiritual eyes, to surround them with truth, and to draw them into His embrace. John 6:44 reminds us, "No one can come to Me unless the Father who sent Me draws him." So we pray for that drawing. We pray for moments of clarity, for divine encounters, for voices of truth to speak into their lives, and for their hearts to respond. Whether our children are toddlers or adults, near to God or far from Him, our prayers for their salvation are never in vain.

The Word of God is filled with promises we can pray in faith. Acts 16:31 declares, "Believe on the Lord Jesus Christ, and you will be saved, you and your household." Isaiah 54:13 says, "All your children shall be taught by the Lord, and great shall be the peace of your children." These verses are more than inspirational; they are covenant promises. We can stand on them when circumstances are difficult, when doubts arise, or when progress seems slow. The seed of the Word, once planted in a child's life, is never truly lost. God watches over His Word to perform it (Jeremiah 1:12), and no prayer for salvation goes unheard.

In addition to salvation, we must also pray for wisdom. Wisdom is not the same as intelligence. It is not simply knowledge or good grades; it is the ability to discern truth, make godly choices, and live in alignment with God's design. Proverbs 4:7 says, "Wisdom is the principal thing; therefore get wisdom. And in all your getting, get understanding." If we want our children to walk in stability, purpose, and blessing, then wisdom must be at the center of their lives. And wisdom begins with the fear of the Lord.

"The fear of the Lord is the beginning of wisdom" (Proverbs 9:10). This fear is not terror—it is reverence, honor, and awe. It is the recognition that God's ways are higher than ours and that His Word is the foundation of all understanding. When children are taught to honor God from a young age, they are positioned to receive wisdom beyond their years. But this doesn't happen by accident—it happens through prayer, instruction, and example.

Pray that your children would hunger for wisdom. Pray that they would value truth over popularity, purpose overpressure, and integrity over convenience. Ask God to surround them with wise counselors, to give them discernment in their relationships, and to guide their decisions. James 1:5 promises, "If any of you lacks wisdom, let him ask of God... and it will be given to him." That promise extends to our children when we stand in their gap. And as we pray, God responds—not only by giving wisdom to our children but also by giving us wisdom in how to raise and guide them.

Wisdom protects, directs, and prepares. It enables our children to resist temptation, to choose the right path, and to avoid unnecessary pain. It positions them for favor. Proverbs 3:13–18 speaks of wisdom as a tree of life, more precious than silver or gold. This is the inheritance we desire for our children—not just success in the eyes of the world, but wisdom from above, which is "first pure, then peaceable, gentle, willing to yield, full of mercy and good fruits" (James 3:17).

And then, beyond salvation and wisdom, we pray for destiny. Every child is born with a divine purpose. God does not create randomly. He forms with intention. Psalm 139:16 says, "Your eyes saw my substance, being yet unformed. And in Your book they all were written, the days fashioned for me, when as yet there were none of them." This verse tells us that God has already written the story. Our job as parents is not to write the script but to help our children discover what God has already written.

Praying for destiny is about calling forth what is hidden. It's about speaking life over your child's gifts, dreams, and calling, even when they themselves do not see it. It's about asking God to reveal their unique purpose, to open doors that align with that purpose, and to prepare their hearts to walk in it with humility and courage. Ephesians 2:10 reminds us, "For we are His workmanship, created in Christ Jesus for good works, which God prepared beforehand that we should walk in them." Your child is not an accident. Their life is not random. They are God's workmanship, and their destiny is part of His plan.

Destiny does not mean fame, fortune, or status—it means faithfulness. It means walking in step with the Spirit, living a life that glorifies God, and making an eternal impact in whatever sphere of life God assigns. Some children may be called to ministry, while others may be called to business, education, healthcare, the arts, or parenting. All of it is holy when done unto the Lord. Our role is to pray that our children hear God's voice, that they walk in obedience, and that they are protected from distractions and detours that would steal their focus or rob their inheritance.

Praying for destiny also means trusting God's timing. Sometimes, it seems like progress is slow or the purpose is unclear. But God is never late. He is always working behind the scenes, preparing both the person and the path. Isaiah 30:21 promises, "Your ears shall hear a word behind you, saying, 'This is the way, walk in it.'" As parents, we pray that our children will recognize that voice, follow it, and never look back.

We must also model this in our own lives. Children are watching us to see if we believe what we pray. They listen to our declarations. They absorb our attitudes. When they see us trust God for salvation, wisdom, and destiny, not just for them but for ourselves; they are more likely to do the same. Our prayers must be matched with lives of faith. Not perfect lives, but lives surrendered to the One who holds it all together.

Prayer is never wasted. Whether whispered in the early morning, cried through tears in the night, or spoken with bold faith in the middle of life's storms—every prayer for your child is a seed. Some seeds sprout quickly; others take time. But God is faithful. Galatians 6:9 tells us not to grow weary in doing good, "for in due season we shall reap if we do not lose heart." The harvest will come.

Keep praying. Keep declaring. Keep believing. Pray for your children's salvation—not as a distant hope, but as a present promise. Pray for wisdom—not just for decisions, but for their entire way of life. And pray for destiny—not according to your plan, but according to God's. Because when we pray in alignment with His will, we can be confident that He hears—and that He will answer in ways far greater than we can imagine.

Chapter 14

Restoration and Reconciliation

Every family has moments of brokenness. Whether through words that wound, seasons of rebellion, loss of trust, or years of silence, the road of parenting is often marked by heartbreak as much as by joy. Yet amid the pain, God's promises shine brightest. He is not only the God of beginnings; He is the God of restoration. He redeems what is lost. He reconciles what has been divided. And He does not do it reluctantly. He delights in restoring families.

There is no situation too fractured, too far gone, or too hopeless for His hand to reach. The Bible tells us in Joel 2:25, "So I will restore to you the years that the swarming locust has eaten." That verse is not a poetic exaggeration; it is a divine guarantee. God can restore what was lost or stolen. He can breathe life into what appears dead. He can rebuild bridges that have long since collapsed.

Restoration begins in the heart of God. Before we even know there is damage, He already has a plan to repair it. He is the Father who watches the road, waiting for the prodigal's return. He is the Shepherd who leaves the ninety-nine for the one. He is the Master Potter, shaping marred vessels into vessels of honor. His nature is redemptive. And His desire is not merely to patch things together—it is to make them new.

As parents, we carry not only the longing but also the authority to call for restoration in our families. When we pray, we are not hoping for a miracle; we are aligning with the very will of God. Colossians 1:20 tells us that God made peace "through the blood of His cross, by Him to reconcile all things to Himself." That includes relationships between parent and child. Through the cross, reconciliation is not only possible but also promised.

Sometimes, that restoration is internal. A child may be physically present but emotionally distant. There may be barriers that words cannot break through. But the Holy Spirit can. He is the Comforter, the Revealer, the One who knows the deep things of the heart. He speaks to places we cannot reach. When we invite Him into the broken places—our own or our children's—He does the work we cannot. Psalm 34:18 assures us, "The Lord is near to those who have a broken heart." No heart is too hardened, and no distance too wide for His reach.

At other times, restoration must begin within us. Parenting exposes our weaknesses. Our failures become glaring. Guilt can overwhelm us, especially when we look back and see the things we wish we had done differently. However, the cross also covers parents. God is not waiting to punish us for our past; He is waiting to restore us. He wants to break the shame that steals our confidence and reconcile us not only to our children but to ourselves.

Reconciliation is not only about peace; it is about realignment. When a child is estranged, confused, or withdrawn, they often feel displaced spiritually and emotionally. They may not be able to find their way back on their own. But reconciliation restores the connection. It clears the noise, reopens trust, and brings them back into a place of belonging. That's why it is worth fighting for. That's why it's worth praying for even when everything looks lost.

Luke 1:17 speaks of the mission of John the Baptist, who would "turn the hearts of the fathers to the children." That verse echoes the last words of the Old Testament in Malachi 4:6 and reveals the very heart of revival. God's move on the earth has always included restoring generational relationships. The enemy seeks to divide—through busyness, offense, or silence—but God seeks to unite. When the hearts of fathers and mothers turn toward their children, barriers begin to fall. Conversations reopen. Identity is affirmed. And God begins to move.

Reconciliation also requires humility. Sometimes, the first step is simply acknowledging the pain—our own or our child's. It may mean apologizing, listening instead of trying to fix it, and showing up in love even when it isn't received. But every humble act is a seed of restoration. James 4:6 tells us, "God resists the proud but gives grace to the humble." That grace can do in a moment what our efforts could not accomplish in years.

Restoration may not come all at once. It may unfold in stages—a conversation, a shared moment, a softened tone. Don't despise the small steps. They are signs of progress. And even when it seems like nothing is happening, God is still at work. Isaiah 43:19 reminds us, "Behold, I will do a new thing; now it shall spring forth; shall you not know it?" Trust that even in silence, restoration is taking root.

Sometimes, as parents, we carry unresolved pain from our upbringing. We may be trying to raise our children while still processing the effects of our past. But God doesn't just restore forward; He also restores backward. He can mend relationships between adult children and their parents. He can renew what was broken in your childhood. What we bring to Him in surrender, He is faithful to transform.

Forgiveness is at the center of restoration and reconciliation. Whether it's forgiving your child, your spouse, or yourself, forgiveness makes room for restoration to begin. It is not a denial of hurt—it is a release of offense. It is choosing to trust God with what we cannot undo. Colossians 3:13 instructs us, "Even as Christ forgave you, so you also must do." In that space of release, God rebuilds.

Reconciliation does not mean everything goes back to how it was. It means something new begins - something marked by grace, honesty, and love. It means the past no longer dictates the present. It means shame no longer holds the pen. And when reconciliation takes root, it touches more than just the immediate relationship. It strengthens identity. It ignites hope. It reflects the heart of the gospel.

Never stop believing in restoration, no matter how long it's been. God is not bound by time. He is not discouraged by delay. He is patient, persistent, and present. His love never gives up. And He will finish what He started. Philippians 1:6 assures us, "He who has begun a good work in you will complete it until the day of Jesus Christ."

Speak restoration. Pray for reconciliation. Believe in a breakthrough; even if you feel like the only one standing, stand. You are not standing alone. God is with you, and He is faithful. Your family's story is not over. With God, restoration is always possible, and reconciliation is always within reach.

Chapter 15

Discipleship and Writing God's Word on Your Children's Heart

Discipleship is not confined to church programs or formal Bible studies; it begins at home and continues through everyday life. It means walking out your faith in such a way that your children learn to follow Jesus not just by what you say but by how you live. It's a lifestyle of teaching, training, modeling, and living out the gospel in ordinary daily routines. And it's one of the most powerful ways we prepare our children for a lifetime of knowing and following Christ.

From the very beginning, God designed parents to be the primary spiritual influencers in their children's lives. Deuteronomy 6:6–7 instructs us, "And these words which I command you today shall be in your heart. You shall teach them diligently to your children and shall talk of them when you sit in your house, when you walk by the way, when you lie down, and when you rise up." This is the vision of writing God's Word on your children's hearts, not through force, but through steady presence and faithful example.

This process begins with modeling a genuine relationship with God. Children are watching closely. They observe how we respond to stress, how we treat others, how we pray, and how we respond to the Word of God. Our lives are the most effective way to teach them the truth. If we want our children to be people of the Word, we must be people of the Word ourselves. When they see us live by Scripture—not only quoting it but leaning on it, submitting to it, and loving it—they begin to understand its power and value.

Writing God's Word on your child's heart also means intentionally planting Scripture in their memory and conversation. This may include memorizing verses together, displaying Scripture on the walls of your home, praying verses aloud, and turning to the Bible during moments of decision or emotional distress. Psalm 119:11 says, "Your word I have hidden in my heart that I might not sin against You." This hiding is not accidental. It requires intention, repetition, and love. When children begin to carry Scripture in their hearts, they carry God's voice with them wherever they go.

Prayer is a key method for reinforcing God's Word. When you pray Scripture over your child -whether it's for peace, strength, wisdom, or salvation - you are impressing that truth onto their hearts. Your voice becomes a vessel for God's truth. Isaiah 55:11 reminds us that God's Word "shall not return to Me void, but it shall accomplish what I please." Speaking His Word out loud over your children is more than discipline; it is prophecy. It is shaping their identity and destiny according to God's design.

Incorporating God's Word into everyday conversations is another powerful method of discipleship. When your child asks a question or faces a problem, offer Scripture as part of your response, not rigidly or mechanically, but with genuine faith and wisdom. Use God's promises as a compass for making decisions, a source of comfort in times of sadness, and an encouragement in times of fear. In doing so, you're teaching your children to turn to the Word as their first resource, not their last resort.

Worship and praise help reinforce the Word in joyful ways. Singing Scripture-based songs or listening to sound worship music biblically can make truth memorable and alive. Music deeply embeds words in the heart. Many children remember what they sing far longer than what they are told. Worship brings Scripture to life and forms joyful associations with truth. It builds a spiritual atmosphere that is rich and fertile for growth.

Corrective discipline, when administered with grace and guided by Scripture, also helps children understand God's ways. When they disobey or hurt others, using the Bible as a guide not just for rules but also for restoration, it helps them connect God's heart with justice and mercy. Hebrews 12:11 reminds us that correction may be painful at the moment, but it produces the "peaceable fruit of righteousness" in those trained by it. Our discipline, rooted in love and Scripture, teaches our children how to return when they stray.

Stories are powerful tools. The Bible is full of them, and they are particularly effective in reaching a child's heart. Share Bible stories that match the season your child is in—courage, forgiveness, kindness, obedience, trust. Let the heroes of Scripture become their mentors. Let them see the faith of David, the humility of Moses, the obedience of Mary, the endurance of Paul. Let the Word breathe into their imagination. As they begin to connect with Scripture personally, it begins to shape how they see the world and themselves.

Writing God's Word on your children's hearts also means encouraging them to engage it for themselves. Teach them how to read their Bible. Help them find age-appropriate versions or devotionals that suit their needs. Read alongside them and ask questions. Invite them to underline verses, pray over what they read, and share what God reveals to them. As they grow, they will begin to hunger for the Word because they see it as real and relevant—not distant or inaccessible.

Remember, this process takes time. Seeds sown in childhood often bear fruit in later years. Some seasons will feel dry, some children will resist, and some truths may seem to fall flat. But God is faithful. His Word does not return void. Galatians 6:9 reminds us, "And let us not grow weary while doing good, for in due season we shall reap if we do not lose heart." Keep planting. Keep watering. Trust God with the harvest.

In a world filled with opinions, media, and shifting values, there is nothing more stabilizing for a child than the eternal Word of God written on their heart. It becomes their compass in confusion, their anchor in trouble, their sword in battle, and their comfort in sorrow. And it begins with everyday discipleship—a life of faith, presence, and truth.

Let your home be the training ground where God's Word is known, loved, spoken, sung, and lived. Let it be etched on the walls and written on hearts, for when it is, you are not raising children but disciples. You are raising sons and daughters of the King, equipped to walk in wisdom, strength, and truth for all the days of their lives.

Chapter 16
Standing in Faith for Your Children

No matter how young or old your children are or where they stand spiritually, you can stand in faith and pray God's Word over them. Whether they are walking closely with the Lord or wandering in uncertainty, the power of God's Word does not change. He is merciful and faithful, and He watches over His Word to perform it. As we pray Scripture, we align ourselves with the will of God, and in doing so, we stand on a foundation that cannot be shaken.

Romans 10:17 tells us, "So then faith comes by hearing, and hearing by the word of God." When we speak God's promises aloud, especially concerning our children, we are not just speaking hope; we are activating faith. The more we hear the Word, the more deeply it roots itself within us and the stronger our prayers become. That is why it is so important to read the promises of God concerning your children out loud. Let your ears hear them. Let your heart absorb them. Meditate on them until faith rises and overpowers fear.

It is in those moments of uncertainty when we see our children struggling or drifting that our faith must remain unmoved. We cannot allow our feelings or circumstances to lead us away from what God has said. His Word is truth. It does not change with the winds of culture or the rollercoaster of emotion. Hebrews 6:18 assures us, "It is impossible for God to lie." If He said it, He will do it. Isaiah 55:11 declares, "So shall My word be that goes forth from My mouth; It shall not return to Me void, But it shall accomplish what I please, And it shall prosper in the thing for which I sent it."

When you open your Bible and pray God's Word over your son or daughter, you are agreeing with God Himself. You are declaring, "Let it be done on earth as it is in heaven." And when you do that, heaven responds. Jeremiah 1:12 reveals God's eagerness: "Then the Lord said to me, 'You have seen well, for I am ready to perform My word.'"

This confidence in prayer grows as we remember that the Bible is God speaking to us personally. These are not distant, abstract promises, they are intimate, living truths meant to shape your family. First, John 5:14–15 affirms, "Now this is the confidence that we have in Him, that if we ask anything according to His will, He hears us. And if we know that He hears us, whatever we ask, we know that we have the petitions that we have asked of Him."

The Word is God's will, and when we pray His Word, we are praying in full agreement with heaven. Isaiah 43:26 says, "Put Me in remembrance; Let us contend together; State your case, that you may be acquitted." When we pray Scripture, we are not informing God of something He has forgotten; we are agreeing with what He has already declared. And He invites us into that place of bold remembrance.

Here are just a few of the promises we can stand on:

Isaiah 49:25: "For I will contend with him who contends with you, and I will save your children."

Isaiah 54:13: "All your children shall be taught by the Lord, and great shall be the peace of your children."

Isaiah 44:3–4: "I will pour My Spirit on your descendants, and My blessing on your offspring."

Psalm 102:28: "The children of Your servants will continue, and their descendants will be established before You."

Jeremiah 31:16–17: "Your work shall be rewarded… and your children shall come back from the land of the enemy. There is hope in your future."

Acts 16:31: "Believe on the Lord Jesus Christ, and you will be saved, you and your household."

Proverbs 11:21: "The seed of the righteous shall be delivered."

Psalm 115:14–15: "The Lord shall increase you more and more, you and your children."

Psalm 112:1–3: "His descendants will be mighty on earth... the generation of the upright will be blessed."

Proverbs 20:7: "The righteous man walks in his integrity; His children are blessed after him."

All of these are yes and amen in Christ. As 2 Corinthians 1:20 reminds us, "For all the promises of God in Him are Yes, and in Him Amen, to the glory of God through us."

When you don't know how to pray, open the Word. Speak the promises. Declare them boldly. Let them build your confidence. Then pray from that place of certainty, trusting that God hears you.

Here is an example of how I've prayed God's Word over my children. May it bless and encourage you and serve as a model for your prayers:

Father, I come to You in the name of Jesus. I thank You that Your Word is sharper than any two-edged sword and is an unstoppable weapon against Satan. I declare Your Word over my (son/daughter) right now. I declare by faith that (Child's Name) will have a quick, repentant heart (Psalm 51:1–3), that their life will bear the fruit of the Spirit (Galatians 5:22–23), that they will trust in You for direction (Proverbs 3:5–6), and that they will live by the Spirit and not gratify the desires of the flesh (Galatians 5:16).

Father, I thank You for saving my children (Isaiah 49:25). I thank You that (Child's Name) is taught by the Lord and has great peace (Isaiah 54:13), that (Child's Name) is established in righteousness, that angels are encamped about them to keep them safe in all their ways (Psalm 91), and that no weapon formed against them will prosper (Isaiah 54:17).

I thank You that (Child's Name) is the head and not the tail, blessed in the city and blessed in the country (Deuteronomy 28:1–13), that their delight is in the Word of the Lord, that they hunger and thirst after righteousness, and that whatever they put their hand to will prosper (Psalm 1:1–3).

Father, I ask that You give (Child's Name) the spirit of wisdom and revelation in the knowledge of You and that You would grant them an understanding heart. That they are being strengthened with might by Your Spirit in their inner man, that Christ dwells in their heart through faith, and that they are being rooted and grounded in Your love. That they may know the love of Christ which surpasses knowledge, and that they be filled with all the fullness of God (Ephesians 1:17–23; 3:14–21).

Thank You for the promises of Your Holy Word. You have said Your Word will not return void but will accomplish what You send it to do (Isaiah 55:11). To You be all glory and praise forever. I ask and believe these things in Jesus' name. I thank You and praise You that now my joy is full (John 16:24). In Jesus' name, Amen.

Let this kind of prayer strengthen your heart. Let it remind you that God is faithful. And never forget: when you stand in faith and speak His Word, you are standing on promises that cannot fail.

Chapter 17
Anchored in His Promises—Hope for Our Children

For every parent who has wept over a wandering child, agonized in prayer over a wayward path, or simply held dreams in their heart for their child's future, the promises of God offer a lifeline of unshakable hope. Amid the swirling chaos of the world and the ever-changing challenges of raising children, the Word of God anchors us in something eternal, trustworthy, and full of peace. God's promises are not empty reassurances; they are covenants sealed in His character, and they remain the surest foundation upon which parents can stand.

God, who formed our children in the womb, who ordained their days before one of them came to be, has not left us to figure it all out on our own. He has made promises, and in them is our confidence. In Jeremiah 29:11–13, He declares: *"For I know the thoughts that I think toward you, says the Lord, thoughts of peace and not of evil, to give you a future and a hope. Then you will call upon Me and go and pray to Me, and I will listen to you. And you will seek Me and find Me, when you search for Me with all your heart."* These words were not spoken in a time of peace and prosperity. They were written to a people in exile, carried away to Babylon, stripped of their home, and facing an uncertain future. Yet it was in that very setting that God promised a future filled with hope. That same promise extends to you and your children even in seasons of exile, in wilderness wanderings, in the waiting.

God's thoughts toward your children are not evil. They are thoughts of peace. They are filled with divine intent and loving purpose. Even when your child's current path seems broken or shadowed by poor choices, God's thoughts are unchanging. He is not shaken by the rebellion of youth or the cold silence of spiritual indifference. He sees what we cannot. He sees the whole story from the beginning to the end. And in His eyes, there is a hope-filled future written for every child, no matter where they are today.

When we come to God in prayer, we are stepping into that promise. He says, *"You will call upon Me and go and pray to Me, and I will listen to you."* There is never a wasted prayer for your child. Every word whispered through tears, every groan too deep for words, every desperate cry in the night is heard. Not only does He hear—He listens. God is not distant or inattentive; He is actively engaged in our prayers. He is near to the brokenhearted and especially attentive to the prayers of a parent interceding for their child. When you pray, Heaven listens. When you seek, you find—not because you are perfect, but because He promised you would when you search for Him with all your heart.

It is often in the long process of seeking that faith is formed. Parents are sometimes required to walk by faith and not by sight for years. But your prayers do not disappear. They accumulate before the throne of God. They are like incense—sweet, persistent, rising, and powerful. Some prayers are answered quickly, others unfold slowly over time, and still others are preserved for a future moment when God's perfect timing is revealed. But rest in this: no heartfelt plea is ever wasted. No prayer goes unnoticed by God.

As we pray for our children, whether they are toddlers or grown adults, the promise of **Isaiah 49:25** gives us boldness and courage. *"For I will contend with him who contends with you, and I will save your children."* What a stunning declaration from the Lord. He is not indifferent to the forces that war against your family. He takes it personally. He enters the battle. God is not a passive observer; He is an active defender of your household. Whatever spiritual, emotional, or physical battle your children may be facing, God steps in as your Advocate and theirs. He contends with the enemies of their soul. He intervenes where you cannot.

This is not a promise that life will be easy, but it is a promise that we are not alone in the fight. Parents often feel powerless in the face of addiction, peer pressure, mental health struggles, and spiritual confusion. But God is not powerless. He will contend. He will step into the courtroom, the school hallway, the inner thoughts of a tormented heart, and He will save. That saving work may come through deliverance, through people He sends, divine encounters, or quiet moments of revelation that no one sees but Him. Still, the promise remains: *"I will save your children."*

There is no limit to the reach of God's arm. No depth too low, no distance too far. He sees the prodigal in the far country. He hears the whispered doubts in the mind of a questioning teen. He knows the secret pain behind your child's eyes that even you cannot fully understand. And still, He saves. He has marked your children. They are not forgotten. They are not forsaken. They are not lost to Him.

In Isaiah 54:13–14 (NJKV), God offers yet another radiant promise: *"All your children shall be taught by the Lord, and great shall be the peace of your children. In righteousness, you shall be established; you shall be far from oppression, for you shall not fear; and from terror, for it shall not come near you."* These words speak to the spiritual legacy of every believing parent. God Himself claims the role of a teacher in your children's lives. While we labor to model faith and impart wisdom, He is working from within. He teaches through His Spirit, His Word, and every avenue of grace. Your children are not only being taught by your example—God is teaching them.

What a comfort to every parent who worries they're not doing enough. While we must be diligent and faithful, we are not alone in shaping our children's hearts. The Holy Spirit is active in them, even when we don't see immediate evidence. He is whispering the truth when they lie awake at night. He is reminding them of the Scripture they heard in Sunday school. He is drawing them, convicting them, comforting them, and guiding them. He is always near, always teaching, always loving.

And the fruit of His teaching is *peace*. "Great shall be the peace of your children." Not just a fleeting calm but a deep, abiding peace that passes understanding. In a world of anxiety, confusion, and chaos, this peace becomes a shield. Even if your child is in a turbulent season,

God's promise of peace stands. There is no expiration date on His promises. If they're not walking in peace yet, hold on—He's not finished. His word will not return void.

The next verse offers assurance for the parents themselves: *"In righteousness you shall be established."* God calls you to stand firm, not in fear or guilt, but in righteousness. He has made you righteous in Christ, and that righteousness is your platform for confident prayer and parenting. You don't have to be perfect to be effective. You just have to be anchored in Him.

Fear may try to creep in. Oppression may knock at your door. But the Lord declares, *"You shall be far from oppression, for you shall not fear; and from terror, for it shall not come near you."* The enemy wants to torment you with fear over your children—fear of failure, fear of harm, fear of spiritual loss. But God says that fear has no place in your heart. His perfect love casts out fear. He surrounds you with His presence and promises you protection from the terror that tries to unravel your peace.

So, what do you do when the waiting is long, when your child seems far from God, or when the pain of watching them struggle feels overwhelming? You return to the promises. You rehearse them in prayer. You speak them aloud in your home. You write them on sticky notes and put them on mirrors. You stand on them again and again, no matter what you see. Because His Word is truer than your circumstances. His promises are stronger than your fears.

Declare over your children: *"God has a future and a hope for you. He is thinking peaceful thoughts toward you. He will answer when I call. He will save you. He will teach you. You will have peace. You are not forsaken. You are not lost. You are deeply loved."* Say it out loud. Say it often. Speak life over them. Bless them with your words. Your voice, filled with faith, can become an echo of God's heart in their lives.

Parenting with hope does not mean denying the difficulties. It means refusing to surrender to despair. It means choosing to see with the eyes of faith. It means believing that God is not done. It means trusting that His promises are personal, powerful, and permanent. He is not a man who should lie. He will do what He said He would do as you walk by faith and not by what you see or feel.

So, take heart, beloved parent. If your child is thriving in their walk with God, keep praying. Keep sowing. Keep trusting. And if your child is far away spiritually, emotionally, or even physically, take heart all the more. These promises are for you. They are alive. They are yours. God's Word is a seed, and when planted in faith, it will bring forth fruit. Maybe not today. Maybe not tomorrow. But in the fullness of time, you will see the goodness of God in your child's life.

Hold fast to the hope that does not disappoint. He who promised is faithful. He sees your heart. He sees your children. And He is working right now in ways you cannot see. Your prayers are powerful. Your faith matters. And your children, no matter where they are, are never out of God's reach.

Thus says the Lord: "Refrain your voice from weeping, and your eyes from tears; for your work shall be rewarded," says the Lord, "and they shall come back from the land of the enemy. There is hope in your future," says the Lord, "that your children shall come back to their own border." These words from Jeremiah 31:16-17 (NKJV) carry the very heartbeat of God for parents who have labored in prayer and cried in anguish over the spiritual condition of their children. There are few pains as deep and enduring as the ache of a parent watching a child walk away from the Lord. Whether it comes in the form of rebellion, addiction, unbelief, or simply a slow drifting away from faith, it cuts to the core. But into that heartbreak, God speaks a powerful, personal word of promise, one that still resonates with power today: "Your work shall be rewarded," and "They shall come back."

To every mother and father who has knelt by the bed at night whispering the names of sons and daughters in prayer; to every parent who has watched with tear-filled eyes as their child spirals down a path of destruction; to every believer who has clung to faith while the prodigal wandered far from home, this word is for you. God has not turned a deaf ear to your cry. He has not dismissed your labor in prayer. He sees. He hears. And He promises that your children are not forgotten.

God's instruction to "refrain your voice from weeping, and your eyes from tears" is not a call to deny your emotions or pretend everything is fine. It is an invitation to shift from sorrow to hope, not because the situation is easy, but because He is faithful. His assurance is not grounded in how things look but in who He is. The promise that your work "shall be rewarded" is not vague or distant. It is a divine guarantee that your prayers, your tears, your fasting, your love, and your patient endurance are not in vain. God is working behind the scenes in ways you cannot see. Even when your child is far off emotionally, spiritually, or physically, God is reaching, calling, and drawing them.

He declares with authority, "They shall come back from the land of the enemy." This is not a poetic metaphor. It is a declaration of victory. Wherever the enemy has taken your child, be it into bondage, confusion, darkness, or despair, God says they will return. Not might, not could, not maybe, but shall. This word is the anchor of your soul. This is the truth to declare over your children when every report and every circumstance says otherwise. The enemy does not get the final word over your child. God does.

God never promised parenting would be painless, but He does promise that He is present and powerful in the process. Some parents wrestle with guilt, wondering if their child's choices are somehow their fault. But while mistakes are part of every family's story, they are not the end of the story. God is greater than our failures, stronger than rebellion, and more faithful than we could ever be. His grace can cover what we cannot control. And His Spirit can reach where we cannot go.

Isaiah 44:3-4 (NKJV) adds even more depth to this hope. "For I will pour water on him who is thirsty, and floods on the dry ground; I will pour My Spirit on your descendants, and My blessing on your offspring," God speaks here not only of personal renewal but generational restoration. The dry ground—your child's heart that seems closed, hardened, indifferent—can be drenched by the floods of the Holy Spirit. When the Lord pours out His Spirit, it is not in small doses. It is in floods. Overwhelming, saturating, life-giving floods.

Your child may seem uninterested in God right now. They may have rejected all they were taught, walked away from the church, or chosen paths that broke their hearts. But the promise still stands: "I will pour My Spirit on your descendants." Not just a gentle sprinkle but a powerful outpouring. God specializes in resurrecting what seems dead. He speaks to dry bones and causes them to live again. He speaks to lost sons and brings them home. And He promises that His blessing will rest on your children, not because they've earned it, but because you've asked for it in faith and because He is a covenant-keeping God.

Isaiah continues, "They will spring up among the grass like willows by the watercourses." The willow is a tree that grows quickly and thrives near streams. Its roots go deep into the soil, drawing water from the source that feeds it continuously. What a picture of your children when the Spirit of God touches them! They will not be stunted or struggling; they will grow, flourish, and thrive in the presence of God. They will rise strong and fruitful, their lives transformed by grace.

This is God's heart for your family. He is not done with your children. The story is not over. The prayers you have prayed are seeds in the ground. The tears you've cried have not gone unnoticed. Psalm 56:8 reminds us that God collects every tear in a bottle. Not one prayer, not one cry, not one sleepless night is wasted. God honors the persistence of a praying parent. And His timing, though often mysterious, is perfect.

Sometimes, the journey is long. The prodigal son in Jesus' parable took his inheritance, left home, and wasted it all. The father didn't chase him down or force his return. But he never stopped watching. He never stopped waiting. He never stopped hoping. And when that son "came to himself" and decided to return, the father saw him "while he was still a great way off" and ran to him. That's the heart of our heavenly Father and it's His heart toward your child.

God is preparing a return. Even if you can't see it now, He is working in unseen places. He is softening hearts through circumstances, conversations, and divine interruptions. He is allowing your child to feel the emptiness of life apart from Him. And when the moment comes—whether through crisis or quiet conviction—God will welcome them home, and so will you.

Your role now is to hold on to hope. Don't allow despair to drown out the voice of promise. Speak God's Word over your child. Declare Jeremiah 31:16-17 over their life by name. Say it out loud: "My child will come back from the land of the enemy. There is hope in my future. My work shall be rewarded." When fear whispers that it's too late, respond with faith: "The Lord is pouring His Spirit on my descendants. My children will rise like willows by the watercourses."

Encourage yourself in the Lord, just as David did when all seemed lost. Surround yourself with believers who will stand with you in prayer and faith. Refuse to agree with the lies of the enemy. Instead, agree with the promise of God. If you feel weary, remember Galatians 6:9: "And let us not grow weary while doing good, for in due season we shall reap if we do not lose heart." The season of reaping will come. God's Word cannot return void.

It may help to recall the stories of others who have seen God do the impossible. Many parents have watched with joy as children who once mocked God are now preaching His Word. Testimonies abound of addicts set free; atheists transformed, wanderers returning—not because of human effort, but because someone believed and prayed and never gave up. Let these stories strengthen your resolve. If God did it for others, He will do it for you.

And when the day comes, when your son or daughter returns, when they bow the knee, when they lift their hands in worship, when they finally say, "God, I'm home"—it will all make sense. Every prayer, every sleepless night, every moment of hope against hope will have been worth it. And the glory will go to the One who kept His promise.

God is writing a redemption story for your family. It may look messy right now, but it's not finished. The chapters of rebellion and wandering will give way to pages filled with grace, healing, and restoration. Hold the line. Stay in the place of prayer. Keep your eyes on the promise.

When you feel alone, remember this: God is more invested in your child's future than you are. He loves them even more than you do. His plans for them are good. His power to save is limitless. And His timing is perfect. Trust Him with your child. Rest in His promise. And rejoice in advance, for the return is coming.

Thus says the Lord—yes, to you, dear parent: "Refrain your voice from weeping, and your eyes from tears; for your work shall be rewarded... They shall come back from the land of the enemy. There is hope in your future... your children shall come back to their own border." This is not wishful thinking. This is the Word of the Lord.

You are not powerless, forgotten, or alone. You are a praying parent, and your prayers are powerful. They water the dry ground, call forth floods, and prepare the way for the Spirit of God to move mightily. You are sowing seeds of faith that will yield a harvest. Keep standing, keep trusting, and keep believing.

Because your children are coming home.

Chapter 18
Aligning Our Saying with Our Praying

Words have power. They carry weight in the spiritual realm, and their impact is not limited to the moments we spend in formal prayer. The words we speak when we pray are heard in heaven, but the words we speak when we leave the place of prayer are just as significant. Scripture is clear that life and death are in the power of the tongue (Proverbs 18:21, NKJV) and that what we continually speak reveals what we believe. If our prayers declare trust in God but our daily conversations are filled with doubt, fear, or contradiction, we weaken the very faith we claim to stand on. To live a life of effective prayer, our saying must align with our prayer.

Jesus Himself emphasized the importance of words. In **Matthew 12:36-37 (NKJV)**, He said, "But I say to you that for every idle word men may speak, they will give account of it in the day of judgment. For by your words you will be justified, and by your words you will be condemned." This isn't just about the words spoken in religious settings. It refers to every careless, thoughtless, or unbelieving word. Our words form patterns and those patterns shape our inner life. Prayer, then, is not only what we do in private moments of devotion, but it is the standard that ought to influence all our speech.

When Jesus taught the disciples to pray in **Matthew 6:9-13 (NKJV)**, beginning with, "Our Father in heaven, Hallowed be Your name," He gave them a structure of faith-filled speech. That prayer includes asking for daily provision, forgiveness, protection, and surrendering to God's will. It is not meant to be repeated mindlessly but to shape how we think and speak all day long. Prayer starts a conversation with God that is meant to continue through our attitudes and expressions. When we ask, "Give us this day our daily bread," but then spend the rest of the day worrying aloud about finances, we are saying words that cancel our own prayers. James warned about this kind of inconsistency. In **James 3:10 (NKJV)**, he said, "Out of the same mouth proceed blessing and cursing. My brethren, these things ought not to be so."

Jesus continually taught that words reflect the condition of the heart. In **Luke 6:45 (NKJV)**, He said, "A good man out of the good treasure of his heart brings forth good; and an evil man out of the evil treasure of his heart brings forth evil. For out of the abundance of the heart, his mouth speaks." If our prayers are to be effective, they must spring from a heart that is aligned with the Word of God and filled with faith. That same heart must govern our conversations in everyday life. Otherwise, we become double-minded—praying with one voice and speaking something entirely different with another.

The Bible gives many examples of how words influence outcomes. Consider the Israelites in the wilderness. Though they had seen God deliver them from Egypt with mighty signs, they constantly complained and spoke words of doubt and fear. In **Numbers 14:28 (NKJV)**, the Lord said to Moses, "Say to them, 'As I live,' says the Lord, 'just as you have spoken in My hearing, so I will do to you.'" Their negative words sealed their fate. What they repeatedly said became their reality. They spoke death into their own destiny.

In contrast, the centurion in **Matthew 8:8-10 (NKJV)** showed the power of faith-filled words. When Jesus offered to come and heal his servant, the centurion replied, "Lord, I am not worthy that You should come under my roof. But only speak a word, and my servant will be healed." Jesus marveled at this man's faith and said, "I have not found such great faith, not even in Israel!" His understanding of authority and his confident speech aligned with divine truth, and it released healing. When we speak words that agree with God's promises, we open the door for the miraculous.

Even in times of hardship, God calls us to speak life. Paul and Silas, locked in prison, prayed and sang hymns to God. **Acts 16:25-26 (NKJV)** says, "But at midnight Paul and Silas were praying and singing hymns to God, and the prisoners were listening to them. Suddenly, there was a great earthquake... and immediately all the doors were opened, and everyone's chains were loosed." Their words of praise in the darkest hour became the key to freedom—not only for themselves but for others around them.

Proverbs offer consistent wisdom about the power of our words. Proverbs 15:4 (NKJV) states, "A wholesome tongue is a tree of life, but perverseness in it breaks the spirit." Words can build up or tear down; they can uplift or bring down hearts. Our goal as believers should be to speak words that reflect God's character and promises. This means aligning our everyday speech with the things we declare in prayer.

Faith must be consistent in the mouth and the heart. **Romans 10:9-10 (NKJV)** says, "If you confess with your mouth the Lord Jesus and believe in your heart that God has raised Him from the dead, you will be saved. For with the heart, one believes unto righteousness, and with the mouth, confession is made unto salvation." Salvation itself comes through this alignment. The heart believes, and the mouth confirms it. This same principle applies to every area of Christian life. We believe in God's promises, and we speak them—not just in prayer but throughout our lives.

Paul urged believers to let their speech be filled with grace and truth. **Colossians 4:6 (NKJV)** says, "Let your speech always be with grace, seasoned with salt, that you may know how you ought to answer each one." Words have the power to influence others. They can testify to faith or expose doubt. They can encourage the weary or deepen someone's despair. When we spend time in prayer asking God to intervene, to heal, to restore, or to move mountains, we must not undo those requests with complaints, criticism, or confessions of defeat.

Jesus said in **Mark 11:23-24 (NKJV)**, "For assuredly, I say to you, whoever says to this mountain, 'Be removed and be cast into the sea,' and does not doubt in his heart, but believes that those things he says will be done, he will have whatever he says. Therefore, I say to you, whatever things you ask when you pray, believe that you receive them, and you will have them." Notice the emphasis on what we say. Jesus connects saying with praying. If we pray for a mountain to move but then speak as if it's immovable, our words have betrayed our prayer. The heart must believe, and the mouth must agree.

The book of Psalms is filled with examples of aligning words with faith. David, though often in distress, continually spoke of God's faithfulness. In **Psalm 19:14 (NKJV)**, he prayed, "Let the words of my mouth and the meditation of my heart be acceptable in Your sight, O Lord, my strength and my Redeemer." David understood the connection between internal belief and external speech. He asked that both be acceptable before God.

In daily life, believers must guard against careless speech. **Ephesians 4:29 (NKJV)** says, "Let no corrupt word proceed out of your mouth, but what is good for necessary edification, that it may impart grace to the hearers." This applies not only to conversations with others but also to how we speak about ourselves, our future, and the circumstances we face. If our prayer is, "God, I trust You to provide," our speech must not follow with, "I don't know how we'll make it." Doubt-filled declarations undermine faith-filled prayers.

The power of speaking in agreement with prayer is also seen in declarations of praise. **Hebrews 13:15 (NKJV)** says, "Therefore by Him let us continually offer the sacrifice of praise to God, that is, the fruit of our lips, giving thanks to His name." Praise is a form of faith-filled speech that continues the prayer conversation with God throughout the day. It is speaking with confidence, even before the answer comes.

Jesus taught that words matter because they reveal the true state of the soul. In times of pressure, what comes out of our mouths reflects what we truly believe. **Matthew 15:18 (NKJV)** says, "But those things which proceed out of the mouth come from the heart, and they defile a man." This is why it's vital to fill our hearts with the Word of God so that when we speak—in prayer or conversation—our words reflect His truth.

Ultimately, to grow in prayer, we must grow in how we speak. Prayer cannot be a private performance disconnected from public speech. What we pray in secret must be reinforced by what we say in public. Faith is not a moment; it is a lifestyle. And our words are the evidence of what we truly believe.

The believer who learns to align their saying with their praying will walk in greater authority and consistency. They will not sabotage their prayers with doubt or contradiction. Instead, their life will become a continuous echo of faith—from whispered prayer to spoken testimony. This alignment releases power, pleases God, and reflects the image of Christ, who never spoke in contradiction to His communion with the Father. May we be people whose words, both in and out of prayer, always align with the faith we profess.

Chapter 19
The Power of the Parental Blessing

The power of blessing is deeply rooted in the ancient pages of the Old Testament, where words spoken by parents over their children shaped destinies, called forth promises, and transferred covenantal favor from one generation to the next. These blessings were not mere hopeful expressions or poetic farewells; they were declarations of divine intent, anchored in God's covenant with His people and spoken with authority by those whom God had placed in a position of stewardship. Parents who blessed their children did so not out of tradition alone but out of reverence for the God who honors spoken words aligned with His will. Blessings stood as a bridge between heaven and earth in the sacred rhythm of family life, linking generations through prophetic utterance and sacred trust. For today's believing parents, the Old Testament offers a wellspring of wisdom and example for intentionally blessing children with words that echo God's promises and invite His presence into every season of life.

One of the earliest and most formative examples of blessing occurs in Genesis 1:28 (NKJV), where Scripture says, "Then God blessed them, and God said to them, 'Be fruitful and multiply; fill the earth and subdue it.'" God Himself models the act of blessing, coupling it with empowering words. This foundational moment in human history teaches that blessing is not passive—it is creative and life-giving. God's blessing over Adam and Eve was not a vague sentiment; it contained purpose, fruitfulness, authority, and divine mandate. Parents who speak blessing over their children are participating in this divine pattern, calling their children into their God-given identity and purpose with words that carry life and authority.

As the narrative of Genesis unfolds, the blessing takes on even more personal significance. In Genesis 12:2–3 (NIV), God says to Abram, "I will make you into a great nation, and I will bless you; I will make your name great, and you will be a blessing. I will bless those who bless you... and all peoples on earth will be blessed through you." The blessing given to Abram—later Abraham—becomes the foundation of generational blessing. God's words to Abraham are not only about him but about his descendants, who will inherit a legacy of favor. This introduces a powerful truth for parents: blessings are generational. What is spoken in faith today can shape generations tomorrow. When parents speak God's promises over their children, they are not only blessing their present but prophesying over their future.

In Genesis 17:7 (ESV), God affirms this generational principle, saying, "And I will establish my covenant between me and you and your offspring after you throughout their generations for an everlasting covenant, to be God to you and your offspring after you." The blessing of God is never meant to stop with one person. It is designed to be passed down, spoken aloud, and sealed with faith. Parents who understand this do not wait for special ceremonies or milestone events; they cultivate a lifestyle of blessing, using everyday moments as opportunities to remind their children of who God is and who they are in Him.

One of the most vivid expressions of parental blessing is found in Genesis 27, where Isaac blesses Jacob. Though the circumstances are complicated by deception, the narrative reveals the weight of spoken blessing. Genesis 27:28–29 (NKJV) records Isaac's words: "Therefore may God give you of the dew of heaven, of the fatness of the earth, and plenty of grain and wine. Let peoples serve you, and nations bow down to you." These words, though spoken under mistaken identity, could not be undone. Once released, the blessing took root. This underscores a critical truth: spoken blessings are irrevocable. They hold power and permanence, especially when uttered from a heart of faith. Parents who bless their children must understand the authority they hold in their words. When spoken in alignment with God's heart, blessings set spiritual direction and invite heaven's resources into a child's life.

The example of Jacob continues this legacy of intentional blessing. As he prepares for his death, Jacob gathers his twelve sons to speak over each of them. Genesis 49 is a powerful chapter, rich with imagery and specificity. Each son receives words tailored to his character, destiny, and calling. Genesis 49:25–26 (NIV) contains Jacob's blessing over Joseph: "…because of your father's God, who helps you, because of the Almighty, who blesses you with blessings of the skies above, blessings of the deep springs below, blessings of the breast and womb. Your father's blessings are greater than the blessings of the ancient mountains…" This blessing is poetic, prophetic, and deeply spiritual. It affirms Joseph's journey and future. Jacob does not merely comment on Joseph's past; he declares God's favor for what is to come. For modern parents, this provides a clear model. Blessings should speak to identity, destiny, and the involvement of God. They are not generic wishes but Spirit-led affirmations of God's promises.

The role of blessing extends beyond family into national identity. In Numbers 6:24–26 (NKJV), God instructs Moses to teach Aaron and his sons how to bless Israel: "The Lord bless you and keep you; the Lord make His face shine upon you, and be gracious to you; the Lord lift His countenance upon you, and give you peace." This priestly blessing, still cherished today, provides a blueprint for blessing that encompasses protection, favor, grace, presence, and peace. Parents who adopt this model in their speech over their children are declaring divine covering over every area of life. Each phrase in this blessing calls down a facet of God's character onto the child. It invites the fullness of God into the heart, home, and future of the next generation. Spoken regularly, this blessing becomes not just a memory but a mantle.

Another profound example appears in Deuteronomy 28, where Moses outlines blessings for obedience. While these blessings are given corporately to Israel, they carry principles that parents can speak personally. Deuteronomy 28:3–6 (NIV) says, "You will be blessed in the city and blessed in the country. The fruit of your womb will be blessed… You will be blessed when you come in and blessed when you go out." These are comprehensive blessings, covering location, family, and daily movement. Parents who personalize these declarations for their children are teaching them that God's blessings are not confined to sacred spaces or religious activities. They follow the obedient and the faithful wherever they go. Speaking such blessings imparts confidence that God is involved in every detail of life.

The wisdom literature also contains powerful affirmations about the value of blessing. In Psalm 127:3 (ESV), the psalmist writes, "Behold, children are a heritage from the Lord, the fruit of the womb a reward." When parents speak this over their children, they are shaping how the child sees themselves, not as burdens, mistakes, or inconveniences, but as divine gifts. This type of blessing instills dignity and worth. Children thrive when they believe they are cherished. Words have the ability to inscribe identity into the heart of a child. When that identity is linked to God's value system, it becomes a shield against lies and insecurity.

In Genesis 48, another moment of blessing takes place as Jacob blesses the sons of Joseph: Ephraim and Manasseh. Genesis 48:15–16 (NKJV) records Jacob's words: "God, before whom my fathers Abraham and Isaac walked... bless the lads; let my name be named upon them, and the name of my fathers Abraham and Isaac; and let them grow into a multitude." This blessing is multi-dimensional. It connects the children to their spiritual heritage, invokes the presence of God, and declares fruitfulness over their lives. Parents today can speak similar blessings, calling their children into spiritual legacy, naming them with the promises of the faith, and declaring multiplication—not merely of possessions, but of godly influence and fruit.

The prophet Isaiah also echoes God's heart for blessing children. In Isaiah 44:3 (New King James Version), God says, "For I will pour water on him who is thirsty, and floods on the dry ground; I will pour My Spirit on your descendants, and My blessing on your offspring." This prophetic promise reveals that God desires to bless not only the current generation but the next. Parents can take these words and turn them into a spoken blessing: "May God pour His Spirit on you and bless you richly." Such declarations align a parent's voice with the voice of God and create a spiritual atmosphere where faith can flourish.

In the Torah, God's desire to bless His people and their children is never distant. In Deuteronomy 30:19 (NIV), Moses says, "This day I call the heavens and the earth as witnesses… that I have set before you life and death, blessings and curses. Now choose life so that you and your children may live." The implication is clear: blessings are connected to choices, and words play a part in shaping both. When parents choose to speak life, to bless rather than curse, they are modeling godly decision-making. They are not only securing blessings for themselves but for their children, reinforcing that the spoken word is a tool for life.

Proverbs, though often associated with warnings and instruction, also reinforce the connection between speech and legacy. Proverbs 20:7 (New King James Version) states, "The righteous man walks in his integrity; his children are blessed after him." The blessing follows the life of the parent, and the words that flow from such a life carry weight. When a parent walks in righteousness and speaks from a place of integrity, their blessing is more than wishful thinking—it is the overflow of a life rightly aligned with God. Children who grow up hearing consistent, godly speech are more likely to internalize and imitate it.

The Old Testament reveals that blessing is not reserved for deathbed moments or major life transitions. In fact, it is a daily opportunity. Psalm 128:1–2 (NKJV) says, "Blessed is every one who fears the Lord, who walks in His ways. When you eat the labor of your hands, you shall be happy, and it shall be well with you." Speaking such truths over children—affirming that fearing the Lord brings happiness and wellness—grounds them in the reality of divine cause and effect. Blessings remind children that God is personal, involved, and responsive.

In all these examples, one consistent theme emerges: blessings are intentional, spoken, and sacred. They are not random expressions but deliberate acts of faith. Parents who speak blessings over their children are echoing heaven, aligning with the covenant, and shaping the spiritual climate of their home. They are not trying to manipulate outcomes but trusting God's Word to do its work. Though ancient, the blessings of the Old Testament remain alive with power today. They build identity, establish purpose, and call forth destiny when spoken with reverence and love. They are one of the most powerful tools a parent has to release God's promises into their children's lives.

Chapter 20
They Shall Come Back: Hope for Every Praying Parent

Thus says the Lord: "Refrain your voice from weeping, and your eyes from tears; for your work shall be rewarded," says the Lord, "and they shall come back from the land of the enemy. There is hope in your future," says the Lord, "that your children shall come back to their own border" (Jeremiah 31:16–17, NKJV). These words are more than poetic encouragement; they are God's covenantal assurance to every parent who has agonized in prayer for a child who has lost their way. Whether your child has wandered into rebellion, addiction, unbelief, or the slow fade of spiritual coldness, these verses pulse with divine hope. They are filled with promise, authority, and the unmistakable voice of a God who restores.

To the parent who whispers their child's name at night with trembling lips, to the one who has grown weary from watching and waiting—to you, this Word is personal. It comes directly from the heart of the Father. He has counted every tear you've shed. He has seen your intercession. He knows the weight you carry. And He speaks directly to it with this divine assurance: "Your work shall be rewarded." Your love, your consistency, your tears, your prayers—they are not in vain. They are seeds planted in faith, and God will honor them.

When the Lord says, "Refrain your voice from weeping," He is not belittling your sorrow. He is not asking you to ignore the pain or to stuff your emotions into silence. He is inviting you to shift your posture from grief to trust. He is calling you out of despair and into hope—not because everything has changed yet, but because He has already spoken. He says there is hope in your future. That is not a wish. That is a decree. When God declares hope, it is anchored not in circumstances but in His unchanging faithfulness.

The phrase, "They shall come back from the land of the enemy," is a declaration of spiritual warfare and victory. God does not say your child might come back or that it's possible under ideal conditions. He says they shall. These words break chains of despair and call forth the power of persistence. The land of the enemy may look different for every child—bondage, confusion, bitterness, false ideologies—but it is the same to God: it is foreign ground, and He will not allow your child to remain there indefinitely.

Jesus illustrated this beautifully in the parable of the prodigal son in **Luke 15 (NKJV).** The son left with arrogance and rebellion, squandered his inheritance, and found himself in a pigsty. But while he was still a long way off, the father saw him, ran to him, embraced him, and restored him. That father had never stopped watching. He never gave up hope. He didn't chase the boy, but neither did he close the door. His heart remained open, his eyes scanning the horizon. This parable isn't just a story; it's a revelation of God's posture toward your child.

And let us not forget that even in God's perfect creation, His first children—Adam and Eve—rebelled. Parental heartbreak does not equal parental failure. You may ask, "What did I do wrong?" but be reminded that your child, like all of us, has free will. God is a Redeemer. His grace covers what you could not foresee. He is more than able to reach into the darkest places, beyond your reach, and bring your child home.

In **Isaiah 44:3–4 (NKJV),** God speaks again to the heart of every interceding parent: "For I will pour water on him who is thirsty, and floods on the dry ground; I will pour My Spirit on your descendants, and My blessing on your offspring." This isn't a light misting of grace; it's a torrential outpouring. The dry ground of your child's heart—the spiritual barrenness, the pride, the bitterness—can be overcome by the flood of the Holy Spirit. When God pours out His Spirit, it transforms. It revives. It awakens. And it never leaves things the same.

The New Testament gives us stories that show this very outpouring. One of the most moving is found in **Mark 9:17–27 (NKJV).** A

101

desperate father brings his demon-possessed son to Jesus. He says, "If You can do anything, have compassion on us and help us." Jesus responds, "If you can believe, all things are possible to him who believes." The father cries out, "Lord, I believe; help my unbelief!" That moment of vulnerable, honest faith moved heaven. Jesus rebuked the unclean spirit and delivered the boy. God honors imperfect faith. He responds to the trembling voice of a desperate parent.

And who could forget Saul of Tarsus? A persecutor of the church, an enemy of the faith. If there was ever a "lost cause," Saul appeared to be it. But God met him on the road to Damascus. In one moment, the persecutor became the apostle. His transformation was so shocking that the early church could hardly believe it. But it reminds us that no heart is too hard, no past too messy, and no mind too deceived for the Spirit of God to reach.

God does not just restore. He redeems. He elevates. He multiplies. Just like the willows mentioned in **Isaiah 44**, your child will not return broken and barren. They will flourish. They will be strong and deeply rooted. They will thrive in the place God plants them. When God restores, He doesn't patch things up—He makes them new.

God sees every tear you've cried. **Psalm 56:8 (NKJV)** says, "You number my wanderings; put my tears into Your bottle; are they not in Your book?" God doesn't just hear your prayers—He records your pain. He values every sigh. Not one tear has been wasted. Each one is evidence of a parent's faith—and God will reward that faith. **Galatians 6:9 (NKJV)** assures us, "Let us not grow weary while doing good, for in due season we shall reap if we do not lose heart."

Look at Peter. He denied Jesus three times. He wept bitterly. Yet Jesus didn't discard him. In **John 21:15–17 (NKJV)**, Jesus gently restores him, asking, "Do you love Me?" three times. With each confession of love, Peter was not only forgiven but recommissioned. Jesus said, "Feed My sheep." Restoration is not just about returning—

it's about reinstating purpose. The same God who restored Peter will restore your child—not only to salvation but to significance.

So what do you do in the waiting? You speak. You declare. You stand on God's promises. Say aloud: "My child shall come back from the land of the enemy. There is hope in my future. My work shall be rewarded." Speak **Isaiah 44:3–4 (NKJV)** over them: "The Lord is pouring His Spirit on my descendants. My children will grow like willows by the watercourses." Let your words match your faith.

Encourage yourself in the Lord as David did in **1 Samuel 30:6 (NKJV).** Refuse to be surrounded by voices of fear and defeat. Instead, partner with believers who will join you in standing on God's Word. Seek out testimonies. Read stories of prodigals returning. Share them. Let them build your faith. If God did it for others, He will do it for you.

The day will come. You will see your child kneel in surrender, raise their hands in worship, and proclaim, "God, I'm home." That day will redeem every sleepless night, every anguished prayer, and every tear shed in faith. The return will be sweeter than the pain. The testimony will be stronger than the trial. And the glory will belong to the One who never stopped pursuing.

God is writing a story of redemption over your family. It may feel messy right now. It may feel like the middle of a storm. But the story is not over. Don't stop reading. Don't stop praying. Don't stop believing. He who began a good work is faithful to complete it.

When you feel weary, trust His strength. When you feel forgotten, know He remembers. When the timeline stretches longer than you hoped, know His timing is perfect. And when the enemy whispers lies, silence them with truth.

This is not wishful thinking. This is the Word of the Lord. "Refrain your voice from weeping... your children shall come back." Keep declaring. Keep believing. Keep standing.

Because your children are coming home.

Chapter Twenty-One: Raising Our Children Inin Love Toto LoveRaising children is one of the most sacred responsibilities God entrusts to a person. It is not merely about managing behavior or ensuring physical well-being but about nurturing the heart, shaping character, and grounding a child in love—both receiving and giving it. From the very beginning, God's design for families has been centered around love. Parents are called to reflect the Father's love and to serve as living demonstrations of His grace, mercy, and truth in the lives of their children. Love is not a parenting strategy; it is the foundation.

The Bible clearly speaks to the atmosphere God desires in the home. Colossians 3:21 says, "Fathers, do not embitter your children, or they will become discouraged" (NIV). This is a profound warning that underscores the power parents have not only over behavior but over the emotional and spiritual formation of a child. A child raised in a home where love is conditional or absent may grow into adulthood carrying wounds that affect every relationship, including their view of God. But when love is the root of all discipline, instruction, and interaction, children are more likely to thrive—spiritually, emotionally, and relationally.

God calls parents to love their children in the same way He loves us: patiently, sacrificially, and unconditionally. 1 Corinthians 13:4-7 (ESV) lays out the standard: "Love is patient and kind; love does not envy or boast; it is not arrogant or rude. It does not insist on its own way; it is not irritable or resentful; it does not rejoice at wrongdoing but rejoices with the truth. Love bears all things, believes all things, hopes all things, endures all things." Parenting with this kind of love means seeing our children not as projects to perfect but as people to serve and shepherd. It means leading with grace even when correction is necessary and showing mercy even in disappointment.

This kind of parenting begins in the heart. Jesus said in Matthew 22:37-39 (NIV), "'Love the Lord your God with all your heart and with all your soul and with all your mind.' This is the first and greatest commandment. And the second is like it: 'Love your neighbor as yourself.'" Our children are our closest neighbors. The command to love them is not implied—it is essential. To love them well, we must first be connected to the source of love. Our relationship with God fuels our ability to love others deeply and genuinely.

The way we love our children teaches them how to love others. It forms their view of relationships, marriage, community, and, ultimately, God. In 1 John 4:19 (NASB), Scripture reminds us, "We love because He first loved us." Children who grow up consistently experiencing love will be more equipped to share it with others. Love teaches empathy, compassion, forgiveness, and strength. It forms the moral compass and emotional resilience that our children will carry into adulthood.

Ephesians 5:1-2 (NIV) gives a model for our behavior: "Follow God's example, therefore, as dearly loved children and walk in the way of love, just as Christ loved us and gave himself up for us as a fragrant offering and sacrifice to God." Parenting is a calling that demands this same self-giving love. It's a daily surrender—to love when we are tired, to give when we feel empty, to remain steady when everything around us is chaotic. And in that sacrificial love, we mirror the love of Christ to our children.

Discipline, when grounded in love, becomes a tool of growth rather than a weapon of control. Hebrews 12:6 (ESV) says, "For the Lord disciplines the one he loves, and chastises every son whom he receives." God's discipline is never to shame but to guide, correct, and restore. Parental discipline must follow the same model. When children understand that discipline comes from love—a desire for their growth and protection—they are more likely to receive it with trust rather than resentment. Love never excuses sin, but it always seeks restoration.

Raising children in love also requires speaking words that build up rather than tear down. Proverbs 18:21 (NIV) reminds us, "The tongue has the power of life and death, and those who love it will eat its fruit." Our words shape identity. Children believe what they hear consistently. Encouraging, affirming, and truth-filled speech helps children see themselves through the lens of God's love and purpose. It equips them with confidence and clarity as they grow.

Jesus was the perfect example of love in action. He welcomed children, blessed them, and made space for them in a society that often overlooked them. In Mark 10:14-16 (NLT), Jesus said, "Let the children come to me. Don't stop them! For the Kingdom of God belongs to those who are like these children. I tell you the truth, anyone who doesn't receive the Kingdom of God like a child will never enter it." Then, He took the children in His arms and blessed them. This is the heart of God toward children, and it must be the heart of every parent.

It is not enough to raise children in a Christian home; we must raise them in Christ's love. This means more than church attendance or Christian rules. It means living out our faith daily in front of them. It means forgiving quickly, repenting sincerely, and loving generously. When children see the gospel lived out—not just preached—they begin to understand its power.

Parenting in love also means creating a home where children feel safe, accepted, and valued. Romans 12:10 (ESV) exhorts us, "Love one another with brotherly affection. Outdo one another in showing honor." This applies to family life. Children who are honored learn to honor others. Homes filled with love and honor become places of healing, growth, and spiritual awakening.

The goal is not to raise perfect children but to raise loved children. Children who know they are deeply loved will be more resilient, more generous, and more open to God. Love softens hearts, builds trust, and opens the door for truth to take root. When parents raise their children in love, they create space for God to move.

Love must be intentional. It must be shown in how we listen, how we correct, how we spend time, and how we serve. Galatians 5:13 (NIV) says, "Serve one another humbly in love." Parenting is service. It is a calling that reflects the servant heart of Jesus. And in that service, love becomes tangible.

We must also teach our children to love others. This is not just moral behavior; it is a spiritual imperative. John 13:34-35 (NIV) records Jesus' words: "A new command I give you: Love one another. As I have loved you, so you must love one another. By this, everyone will know that you are my disciples if you love one another." Children raised in love are more likely to become disciples who love.

Parents who raise their children in love and to love are fulfilling one of the greatest commandments and stewarding one of God's most precious gifts. 1 Peter 4:8 (ESV) reminds us, "Above all, keep loving one another earnestly, since love covers a multitude of sins." Love doesn't eliminate struggles or mistakes, but it gives grace the room to work. It turns failure into learning and conflict into reconciliation.

At the center of every godly home must be the cross—the ultimate demonstration of love. Romans 5:8 (NLT) declares, "But God showed his great love for us by sending Christ to die for us while we were still sinners." This is the message we must live and give to our children. That they are loved, not because of what they do, but because of who God is. This truth sets them free to love others with the same grace.

As parents, we won't always get it right. But love is patient. Love keeps going. And God's love never fails. When we parent in His love and teach our children to walk in it, we are building something that will last far beyond our years.

Faith, hope, and love remain. But the greatest of these is love (1 Corinthians 13:13, NIV). Let this be the legacy we leave in the hearts of our children.

Chapter 22
Training a Child in the Ways of the Lord

God entrusts parents with shaping a child's heart, mind, and soul. In a world that is constantly shifting in its values, definitions, and priorities, God's Word remains steadfast. It provides clear direction, eternal wisdom, and unshakable promises. Among the clearest of these instructions and reassurances for parents and caregivers is found in Proverbs 22:6: "Train up a child in the way he should go; even when he is old he will not depart from it" (ESV). This is not merely wise counsel; it is a promise linked to obedience—a divine principle embodied in the character of a faithful God.

To train a child is far more than enforcing rules or teaching manners. It begins with intentional, day-by-day discipleship. It means introducing them to the heart of God, not just the habits of religion. Children learn what they live, and the tone of the home becomes the soil in which their hearts grow. Training involves more than instruction; it includes modeling, correction, encouragement, and grace. Parents are called to embody what they want their children to emulate. Words matter, but examples shape identity.

The Hebrew phrase "in the way he should go" can also be understood as "according to his way," suggesting an awareness of each child's unique temperament, gifting, and spiritual makeup. God creates every child with divine intentionality. Parenting is not one-size-fits-all. Wise training recognizes the individuality God places in each life. This doesn't dilute the truth of Scripture but rather applies it in ways that connect meaningfully with a child's heart. When we do this in faith, God promises that what is planted will endure. Even if a child wanders, the seeds of truth remain, ready to bear fruit in the right season.

The weight of this responsibility can be overwhelming. No parent does this perfectly. But God never expects perfection; He expects surrender. He promises to partner with us. Psalm 127:3 reminds us, "Children are a heritage from the Lord, offspring a reward from him" (NIV). They are not possessions to control but gifts to steward. We are called to nurture, guide, and release them to God's purposes. It is His Spirit that ultimately draws them and His grace that completes our efforts.

Ephesians 6:4 echoes and expands on the call to raise children with care and intention: "Fathers, do not provoke your children to anger, but bring them up in the discipline and instruction of the Lord" (NASB). This instruction applies to all who influence a child's life. The charge is two-fold: avoid provocation and apply godly discipline. Provoking a child—through harshness, neglect, inconsistency, or criticism—can create deep wounds that distance them from both the parent and God. But when children are raised with loving correction, steady truth, and patient instruction, they are more likely to grow with a secure identity and an open heart.

God does not call us to raise perfect children but to raise children who know the perfect Father. This means leading them to Jesus again and again through our words, our decisions, our forgiveness, and our repentance. When we fail—and we will—our humility and confession become some of the most powerful teaching tools. Children are watching. They are learning not only what to believe but how to believe.

God's promises for our children are rooted in His unchanging nature. Numbers 23:19 declares, "God is not human, that he should lie, not a human being, that he should change his mind. Does he speak and then not act? Does he promise and not fulfill?" (NIV). What He says, He will do. If He promises that training up a child in the way they should go will anchor them for life, then we can trust that even in the waiting, even in the wandering, His Word is still at work.

It is important to understand that God's promises are not formulas. They are not guarantees of ease or proof against rebellion. They are, however, deeply reliable truths tied to His character and authority. Some parents sow in tears, watching their children drift far from what they were taught. And yet, God's promise remains. Isaiah 55:11 assures us, "So is my word that goes out from my mouth: It will not return to me empty, but will accomplish what I desire and achieve the purpose for which I sent it" (NIV). Every Scripture spoken, every bedtime prayer, every moment of godly discipline—these are seeds planted in faith. They do not return void.

Raising children according to God's ways is a long path, not a short sprint. It requires endurance, wisdom, and, above all, love. 1 Corinthians 13:7 speaks powerfully to the posture of the parent's heart: "[Love] bears all things, believes all things, hopes all things, endures all things" (ESV). This is the posture we are to carry in our parenting—believing, hoping, and enduring through every stage, season, and struggle. It is this love, rooted in the gospel, that will echo in the hearts of our children long after they leave our homes.

God is not distant in the process of parenting. He is actively involved, leading, empowering, and encouraging those who call on Him. James 1:5 promises, "If any of you lacks wisdom, let him ask of God, who gives to all generously and without reproach, and it will be given to him" (NASB). What a profound promise to every parent feeling unsure or inadequate. God supplies the wisdom we need, often right in the moment we need it.

Faithful parenting begins with faithful dependence. Our children need more than rules—they need to see a living faith. When they witness parents who pray, worship, forgive, and serve, they begin to understand who God is beyond church walls. And as they grow, they carry that understanding into their own lives. Deuteronomy 6:6-7 gives a clear call: "These commandments that I give you today are to be on your hearts. Impress them on your children. Talk about them when you sit at home and when you walk along the road, when you lie down and when you get up" (NIV). God intends for His Word to be woven into the fabric of family life, not treated as a side topic or Sunday-only activity.

This requires intentional time and intentional teaching. But it also requires joy. Psalm 78:4 says, "We will not hide them from their children, but tell to the coming generation the glorious deeds of the Lord, and his might, and the wonders that he has done" (ESV). Sharing the works of God should be a delight, not a burden. Children respond to joy, and joy is one of the strongest witnesses of authentic faith.

There will be hard days. There will be questions without easy answers, choices that break your heart, and seasons where the fruit of your labor seems invisible. But the promise still stands. Galatians 6:9 urges us, "Let us not become weary in doing good, for at the proper time we will reap a harvest if we do not give up" (NIV). Keep sowing. Keep trusting. Keep praying. God is faithful to His Word.

Every child is ultimately God's. We are caretakers and shepherds for a season. And in that role, we cling to His promises for them and us. Philippians 1:6 gives us assurance in the journey: "Being confident of this, that he who began a good work in you will carry it on to completion until the day of Christ Jesus" (NIV). God begins the work in our hearts and theirs—and He is the one who brings it to full maturity.

Our role is not to control outcomes but to be faithful to our calling. To parent with grace, to teach with truth, and to model with integrity. When we do this, God moves in ways we cannot see. He honors His Word. He draws hearts. He restores what is broken. He redeems what seems lost.

So we stand on Proverbs 22:6 (ESV), not as a wishful thought but as a rock-solid promise: "Train up a child in the way he should go; even when he is old, he will not depart from it." And we obey the charge of Ephesians 6:4 (NASB): "Fathers, do not provoke your children to anger, but bring them up in the discipline and instruction of the Lord."

These verses are not just parenting advice. They are divine invitations. They call us to believe in the God who gave us our children and trust that He works in them even when we cannot see the evidence.

God's promises are not small. They are vast, eternal, and grounded in love. For every parent holding on, hoping, praying—know this: your labor is not in vain. Your children are seen, known, and loved by God. And His promises for them will stand firm, now and forever.

There were years when it felt hopeless. My daughter Audra, at 16, had taken a hard left turn from the path she was raised on. As a single parent, I had done my best to raise my kids in church and teach them God's Word at home. When Audra was little, she had such a sensitive conscience—she once came to me in tears because she tried a cigarette. Back then, I thought we were off to a great start, and I believed the seeds of faith planted early would carry her through life.

I wasn't perfect—I stumbled plenty—but I always tried to model a godly life, quick to repent and keep moving forward. For a while, things looked promising. I even managed to put them in a private Christian school, hoping to surround them with a good foundation. But when tuition costs became too heavy, I had no choice but to move them to public school. That's when things started to unravel. New friends, new influences—not the good kind. Audra started experimenting with pills and pot. I prayed. I fasted. I believed.

When she became pregnant, forgiveness flowed easily. She gave birth to an amazing little boy—now 23 and getting ready to graduate from college. I dug into Scripture like never before, writing down promises about my children and praying them aloud almost daily. I believed faith comes from hearing, so I made sure both God and the devil heard me loud and clear. I enlisted every prayer warrior I knew to pray for Audra and my grandchildren. During those years, Audra had two more children out of wedlock, another fantastic son, and then, several years later, a precious baby girl. I love my three grandchildren with all my heart, but watching my daughter continue down the wrong path was incredibly painful. She loved her children, but years of addiction had warped her thinking, and bad parenting decisions were made.

In 2007, tragedy struck. My son, Audra's brother, was killed in a car accident. Later, Audra told me that the last time she saw him, he had urged her to quit drugs and be the mother she was meant to be. For a moment, it seemed she might listen. She even checked herself into rehab. Hope flickered—only to be crushed within days when she relapsed. Over time, her choices of friends and boyfriends dragged her even deeper into addiction. She wasn't a victim; she had free will, and she was using it poorly. There were arrests, a revolving door of bad influences, and countless heartbreaks. My home became a stop for bail bondsmen, and my wallet unknowingly financed her addiction under the guise of "helping with food and clothes." At one point, I even got a call from the SWAT team asking if I had a key to Audra's house so they could serve a warrant. Nothing quite humbles a parent like seeing your daughter escorted out in handcuffs by the SWAT team.

I had to make hard choices. I stopped paying for her house payment, forcing her to move into an extended-stay hotel. Things only worsened. Eventually, she was sentenced to three months in a court-ordered rehab. She got clean for a while. Then she relapsed again—this time with fentanyl. Despite my warnings, she reunited with her old boyfriend— one of the many poor choices she seemed determined to make.

By this time, I had remarried and moved into my wife's house, while Audra stayed in my old home with her daughter and her boyfriend. I tried setting boundaries—"No boyfriend or you're out!"—but enforcing them was more complicated than setting them. On one particularly heartbreaking visit, Audra was coming down hard from a high and treated me with such disrespect that I drove away sobbing, asking God, "What do I do now?" In my brokenness, I heard Him almost audibly in my heart: "Do you trust Me?" I repented right then for not fully trusting Him and shouted, with all the faith I could muster, "Yes, Lord, I trust You!" That moment felt more real than the car I was driving. I wrote it down in my journal as a memorial stone. Every time the enemy tried to make me worry, I would go back to that moment and remember God's voice.

It had been seventeen long years of prayers, tears, and holding onto hope. God was working even when I couldn't see it. Soon after, someone reported Audra to DHS. Police found multiple types of drugs in her possession, and this time, the court took her daughter away and placed her with a fantastic family we all knew. I didn't bail her out. She spent eight months in jail. During that time, I sold my old house and truly let God take over. Jail turned out to be Audra's turning point. She didn't waste her time there: she graduated from the CSI program (Community-Focused, Safety-Driven, Integrity-Based), attended Bible studies and chapel services, and even mentored other women. God was answering years of prayer.

Today, by the grace of God, Audra has been clean and sober for nearly three years. She is forty years old and attends two to three weekly meetings. She loves the Lord with all her heart. She's working, self-supporting, and building a stable life for herself. Like the prodigal son, she "came to herself," and when she did, I was there with open arms. I didn't kill the fatted calf or give her a ring, but we did give her car back to her!

Twenty years of waiting, praying, questioning, and standing on God's promises was difficult because you're comparing what you can see with the promise that has yet to come to pass. There were many moments when I questioned God about where I had gone wrong or wondered what I did to deserve this. However, I have learned that even children raised in a Christian home can wander. They have their own choices to make. God is patient, merciful, and faithful.

Remember, "Whom the Son sets free is free indeed." All I can do is praise God and give Him ALL the glory. He is faithful, even through the darkest valleys. He is mighty to save. And He is the God who restores what was lost. Parents and Grandparents, no matter how long it's been, do not lose your faith; keep believing because God is at work on your child's heart, and they will come home.

The Prayer I Wrote and Prayed for Years for My Prodigal

Father,

I come to you in the Name of Jesus. I thank you for Your Word, which is sharper than any two-edged sword and is an unstoppable weapon against satan. I declare Your Word over my **(Son/Daughter)** right now. I declare by Faith that **(Child's Name)** will have a quick, repentant heart *(Psalm 51:1-3)*, that **his/her** life will bear the fruit of the Spirit *(Gal 5:22-23)*, that **he/she** will trust in You for direction *(Proverbs 3:5,6)*, and that **(Child's Name)** will live by the spirit and not gratify **his/her** flesh (Gal 5:16). Father, I thank you for saving my children *(Isaiah 49:25)*, I thank you that **(Child's Name)** is taught by the Lord and have Great peace. *(Isaiah 54:13),* that **(Child's Name)** is established in righteousness, that angels are encamped about **him/her** to keep **(Child's Name)** safe in all their ways *(Psalm 91)*, that no weapon formed against them will prosper *(Isaiah 54:17)*. I thank you that **(Child's Name)** is the head and not the tail, they are blessed in the city and blessed in the country *(Deut 28:1-13)*, that **(Child's Name)** delight is in the Word of the Lord, that they hunger and thirst after righteousness and whatever they put their hand to do shall prosper *(Psalm 1:1-3)*. Father, I ask that You give **(Child's Name)** the spirit of wisdom and revelation in the knowledge of You, that You grant them according to the riches of Your glory, and that they are being strengthened with might by Your Spirit in their inner man, that Christ dwells in **(Child's Name)** heart through faith, that they are being rooted and grounded in Your Love, that they will know the love of Christ which passes knowledge, and be filled with Your fullness. *(Ephesians 1:17-23 and 3:14-21)* Thank You for Your promises of Your Holy Word. You have said, "Your Word will not return void but will accomplish that for which you sent it." *(Isaiah 55:11)* To You be glory and praise forever and ever. Father, I ask these things and believe they are done in the

Name of Jesus. I thank You and Praise You that now my joy is full. *(John 16:24)*

Closing Prayer

Heavenly Father,

We thank You for Your unchanging Word and Your everlasting promises. You are the God who sees every tear, hears every whispered prayer, and responds with unfailing love. Thank You for the assurance that You are not only our God—but the God of our children and their children after them.

Lord, we place every child in Your hands—those walking closely with You and those who have strayed. We stand on Your promises that our work shall be rewarded and that our children shall come back from the land of the enemy. We declare in faith that they will rise like willows by the watercourses, rooted and flourishing in Your presence.

We ask You now to pour out Your Spirit on our descendants. Break every chain, soften every heart, and shine Your light into every dark corner of their lives. Call them by name. Draw them with cords of love. Let the seeds of faith planted through prayer, teaching, and example bear a harvest of righteousness.

Help us remain steadfast as parents, grandparents, mentors, and intercessors. When we are weary, strengthen us. When we are discouraged, remind us of what You have spoken. Fill our mouths with Your Word and our hearts with Your peace.

Lord, we rejoice in advance for the testimonies yet to come. We give You glory for the children returning home, the restored lives, and the generations that will declare Your faithfulness.

Let our families be a display of Your covenant love—a light in this generation and the next. We seal every promise in the powerful, matchless name of Jesus Christ. Amen.

If you have never received Jesus as your Lord and Savior, I invite you to pray the prayer below to receive Him. Please pray this prayer out loud and allow the God of Glory to transform your life, make you a permanent and eternal member of His family, and make you a partaker of the Great and Precious promises in His Word.

Heavenly Father,

I come to you in the Name of Jesus. Your Word tells me, "If I come to You, I will not be turned away." So I know You receive me, and I thank You for it. You said in Your Word, "Whosoever shall call upon the Name of the Lord shall be saved." So, I am calling on you, Lord. You also said, "If I confess with my mouth Jesus as Lord, and believe in my heart that God has raised Him from the dead, I will be saved. I believe in my heart God raised Jesus from the dead, and I confess with my mouth Jesus is my Lord, so I believe you have now saved me. And I believe, according to Your Word, I have now become the righteousness of God in Christ.

I am a New Creation in Christ Jesus. The old me has passed away, and I have become new.

Praise You, Lord, and thank You, Lord, for saving me in Jesus's Name.

(Scriptures in this prayer are from the NKJV)

If you or your children prayed this prayer with an open heart or were blessed while reading this book, please let me know through the following email:

✉ **wnelsonauthor@outlook.com**

Note from the Author:

Scripture is at the heart of every chapter in this book. You might notice some verses appear more than once; that's intentional. Each time they're repeated, it's to examine them from a new perspective or apply them to a different situation, helping you understand their meaning more completely.